BRITAIN'S
LOST
TRAGEDIES
UNCOVERED

Also by Richard M. Jones

Non-Fiction

The Great Gale of 1871
Lockington: Crash at the Crossing
The Burton Agnes Disaster
End of the Line: The Moorgate Disaster
Capsized in the Solent: The SRN6-012 Hovercraft Disaster
Royal Victoria Rooms: The Rise and Fall of a Bridlington Landmark
The Diary of a Royal Marine: The Life and Times of George Cutcher
Collision in the Night: The Sinking of HMS Duchess
RMS Titanic: The Bridlington Connections
Living the Dream, Serving the Queen
The 50 Greatest Shipwrecks
When Tankers Collide: The Pacific Glory Disaster
The Farsley Murders

Fiction

Boleyn Gold
Austen Secret

BRITAIN'S LOST TRAGEDIES UNCOVERED

RICHARD M. JONES

The History Press

This book is dedicated to the work of the emergency
services throughout history

First published 2021

The History Press
97 St George's Place, Cheltenham,
Gloucestershire, GL50 3QB
www.thehistorypress.co.uk

British Library Cataloguing in Publication Data.
A catalogue record for this book is available from the British Library.

ISBN 978 0 7509 9661 7

Typesetting and origination by The History Press
Printed and bound in Great Britain by TJ Books Limited, Padstow, Cornwall.

Trees for LYfe

Contents

Introduction   7

1   1837: Southampton Fire   11
2   1861: Great Gale of Whitby   18
3   1869: Hosier Lane Family Massacre   27
4   1893: Sinking of SS *Gwendoline*   35
5   1907: Sowerby Bridge Tram   40
6   1908: Barnsley Public Hall Crush   48
7   1925: Dibbles Bridge Coach Crash (1)   54
8   1927: Hull Rail Disaster   60
9   1939: Sinking of the *Piłsudski*   68
10 1952: Farnborough Air Show   72
11 1957: Isle of Wight Air Crash   79
12 1968: Ronan Point Collapse   84
13 1970: Explosion in the Hull Underpass   90
14 1971: Clarkston Gas Explosion   101
15 1975: Dibbles Bridge Coach Crash (2)   107
16 1976: Fire on HMS *Glasgow*   119
17 1980: Denmark Place Arson Attack   131
18 1981: New Cross Fire   140

19 1984: Abbeystead Explosion   149
20 1985: Dover Hovercraft Crash   160
21 1990: Sinking of the *Flag Theofano*   167
22 1993: Southampton Airport Crash   174
23 1995: Knight Air Flight 816 Crash   179

    Afterword   196
    Acknowledgements   202

Introduction

I was only 11 years old when I started researching disasters, and it was the story of the *Titanic* that fascinated me more than anything else. This led to me reading up on the battleship *Bismarck*, mostly because the same person had found both shipwrecks, and would later go on to find so many more through the years. But, as the forensics of a shipwreck were broken down, I started to be interested in many other disasters. A plane crashed in Pittsburgh in 1994 and the newspaper coverage hooked me, as the investigation drew a blank for many years. The police investigation into major serial killings and the Oklahoma City bombing of 1995 grabbed my attention similarly, and I soon realised that I was inadvertently creating a small archive of information surrounding any kind of investigation into a major tragic event.

As the years went by, I wondered what I was going to do with all the information that I had collected and filed. Sat in a pub in Bridlington, East Yorkshire, one day, I decided to write about the ones that had been forgotten over time. I would start with the one right on my doorstep: the Great Gale of 1871, where around fifty people had been killed and twenty-eight ships wrecked on the beach, just 100yd away from me. This led to me looking into other forgotten disasters, and for each of them I tried (and in some cases succeeded) to put up a memorial; in doing all this I also managed to uncover some fascinating and new information that revealed a completely different story to what was generally known at the time of these events taking place.

'Smaller' disasters tend to get forgotten over time. Everybody knows the names Lockerbie, Hillsborough, Zeebrugge, King's Cross, Dunblane and Hungerford. The names alone lead the typical person to instantly remember what happened there that shocked them so much – a terrorist attack, a ferry capsizing, a major fire – and the fact that these were huge headlines in the papers for years. But, as I studied the forgotten tragedies, I became aware of some incredible stories of bravery that were unrecognised, unanswered questions that people had been too scared to ask, and memorials that had never materialised. Being able to find out something that nobody else had was incredible; to tell the story of these people, to open a memorial and to have the names of once-forgotten victims read out once again at the site of a tragedy made all the efforts by myself and all those who assisted me worthwhile.

It is here that we question – is any disaster really forgotten? It is never forgotten by the survivors who lived through the trauma of seeing people injured and dying. It is never forgotten by the relatives of those who never came home. Look into the past and the information is there, once you dust it off and read it. The police reports, the fire brigade reports, the archives, newspaper articles, the stories from survivors and relatives – the list is endless. But ask the average guy on the street if they remember Lockington and they will likely look blank and suggest you may mean Lockerbie.

So, it is my mission to tell as many stories of these forgotten disasters as possible, so that future generations can learn about what happened and understand what lessons were learned. In this book you will see that lightning really does strike twice, as a coach crash at Dibbles Bridge in 1925 was followed almost fifty years to the day by another, more devastating one, at the exact same spot. The same goes for Sowerby Bridge: an out-of-control tram killed several passengers in 1907; another out-of-control vehicle, this time a truck, did the same just a few yards away in 1993. While we do often learn from mistakes, accidents still happen, and people often take shortcuts.

I have chosen twenty-three disasters around the UK that have occurred within the last 200 years. Some are better remembered, mainly due to the fact they are still within living memory, while others are less well known. I can only hope that this helps us to remember many of those who have been involved in these incidents and highlight facts that would have otherwise been forgotten.

Richard M. Jones
October 2020

1

1837: Southampton Fire

The town of Southampton on the southern English coast is no stranger to trade and industry; in fact, it is the trades ferrying in and out of the well-sheltered port that have made this place such a sought-after ending to a journey on the high seas. Reclassified as a city in 1964, Southampton is most famous for the introduction of ocean liners, which tended to get bigger as the years went by. Even today you can't walk around the city without seeing evidence of the largest ships in the world, particularly that of the *Titanic*, which made her maiden voyage from here in 1912 only to come to a tragic end in the mid-Atlantic.

Not far from where the ships would come alongside lay the warehouses and merchants' houses that would arrange the transportation and sort out costs, fares, legal issues, taxes and so on. King, Witt and Co. were merchants of glass and lead who also traded in oil and sugar, and had a warehouse just 140yd from the quayside at 80 High Street, right at the southern end of the street. Along with the buildings, they also owned two ships, the newly built whaling vessel *Ariel* and the *John Witt*.

The warehouse was a four-storey brick building with a cellar. In addition to a huge amount of sheet and pipe lead, it stored

A flyer giving the public details of the 1837 Southampton fire. (Courtesy Southampton Library)

shot in bags, fifty carboys of turpentine, each of 12 gallons, oil, varnish, wine, paint, glass, brushes, lamp black, resin, bottle wax and almost 200lb of gunpowder. At the back were the stables and hayloft.

With the amount of flammable and combustible material kept in one small area, it would be the worst-case scenario for a fire to erupt in these storage houses. But late in the night of Tuesday, 7 November 1837, that is exactly what happened.

At 23:15 it was noticed that a fire was burning in the hay-loft above the stables but, although people rushed to the scene straight away, it was already too late to do anything about it as the materials stored there caused the fire to spread too quickly. Flames shot off in every direction and within minutes the fire became a raging inferno. The stables were joined to the warehouse by the roof and before long the fire made its way across this and into the main warehouse building.

Fire spread across the upper levels of the warehouse, touching the nearby Royal George Inn and setting the curtains and windows alight. There was a shortage of proper firefighting equipment and, despite its seemingly fortuitous juxtaposition, the water was a major obstacle for those trying to get to the scene of the fire. A human chain was formed to remove some of the other dangerous material to prevent an even bigger disaster, and thankfully a storage of gunpowder and turpentine was moved out of the way; otherwise that would have taken out most of the street and everybody in it. Important paperwork was rescued from the counting house, which opened on to the High Street, and slowly but surely the important items in the business were being saved.

But one by one the bottles of flammable liquids exploded in flames and spread the fire further, running across the floors and leaking through the boards to the rooms and people below.

People from all over the area rushed to the scene and for over an hour they helped where they could, but nothing prepared them for what happened next.

Despite having almost an hour to subdue the fire, the fire brigade was struggling. They had brought three engines with them, but these were poorly equipped; for example, none of them carried anything that could pull down the warehouse roof. The water supply for the warehouse was also inadequate, so they had to send someone to the reservoir 2 miles away to turn on the full supply. By this point, the damage was already too severe to tackle with light machinery and it was about to get worse.

Soon after midnight a series of huge explosions wrecked the front of the building and destroyed internal fixtures, causing parts of the structure to collapse. Fifty people were on the premises at the time and almost all of them were unfamiliar with the arrangement of the building. Many of them were unable to escape, while others jumped out of windows and crawled through the wreckage of the warehouse, the doors having been blown shut by the explosion. Many were buried in the rubble and wreckage, while those who survived suffered horrific injuries from which they would never recover. Most of these victims had nothing to do with the affected company and were simply nearby residents who wanted to stop the fire spreading to other businesses.

The fire was finally brought under control at 04:00 the next day, by which time the buildings were destroyed but the surrounding businesses suffered only slight damage that could be repaired.

When the drama was finally at an end, it was found that seventeen people had died within the building and another five would succumb to their injuries over the coming days. The youngest of these was 16-year-old apprentice butcher George Bell. Bell had been in the warehouse with Richard Young and after the first explosion they had dropped everything and ran quickly, but the collapsing internal structure fell on Bell and he was buried in the rubble. Young escaped but Bell's burned body was recovered later. The oldest victim was 50-year-old stonemason John Harley.

One of the victims was William Oakley, only just married and working as a tailor. He was due to make a return journey back to his wife and child in London that evening after visiting relatives but

The memorial to those lost in the Southampton fire at the bombed-out remains of Holyrood Church. (Author)

was persuaded to stay another day. Another was Edward Ludford, a cooper (maker of barrels and casks) who died eight days after the fire, leaving four children and a pregnant wife.

The charred remains of the victims were laid out at the nearby Fountain Inn; in addition to the twenty-two dead, a total of twenty-four were seriously injured, leaving ninety dependant women and children.

Those who had risked their lives to tackle the fire and rescue survivors were hailed as heroes, but nothing could alleviate the shock of so many deaths in one incident that should never have happened. The heroes of that night were named as Richard Young, W. Jones, William Terry, G. Carr, John Ford, Nathaniel Anderson, John White, H.G. Greeves and William Gouk. They were awarded a medal by the London Society for the Protection of Life from Fire.

Southampton was in a state of shock. The theatre and trading ceased as a mark of respect, with the Mayor, Joseph Lobb, launching an appeal fund to help the survivors and families of the deceased. This eventually totalled almost £7,000, including £100 from Queen Victoria. The fund was split between 101 people: £170 to each of the eight widows, £25 to each orphan (£20 to apprentice them and £5 for when their apprenticeship was over) and £180 to the three most disabled survivors.

An inquest was held and it highlighted the fact that the lack of equipment and the poor state of the town's preparedness for such an incident had cost the lives of twenty-two men. With proper attendance of firemen, it may have been possible to pull down the stable and isolate the fire before it had spread to the warehouse. Of the firemen, the hearing concluded that 'the jury are also of opinion that the supply of water was greatly delayed and the arrangements to obtain it insufficient and improper; that the arrival of the engines was delayed; that the fire department is itself incomplete, particularly in the implements for checking fire and saving life, and the arrangements in many respects defective, especially in the discipline of the firemen'.

The cause of the fire was never found, although fireworks let off recklessly nearby were blamed by many. The owners of the warehouse, Messrs King and Witt, continued to trade despite their insurance not meeting the full cost of their losses, which stood at £12,000.

In July 1838 two large plaques were placed on either side of the door to Holyrood Church listing the names of all the victims as a tribute to the memory of those who perished. Replacements were installed in later years after the near destruction of the church during the Second World War, when Southampton was heavily hit in the bombing raids. The church is now a permanent memorial to the Merchant Navy, the two plaques more prominent than ever.

The site of the fire is unrecognisable today. Modern flats now stand at the location of what was once a trading establishment, the nearby ancient castle walls and vaults giving the only indication of this area's rich history.

2

1861: Great Gale of Whitby

For sailors, the coast of Great Britain has always been both a safe haven and a peril to be faced, with the weather conditions deciding whether a seafarer casts his lines and puts to sea or stays in port where it is safe. But when the good fortune suddenly turns sour and ships become stranded, it is up to the brave townsfolk of the seaside dwellings to risk their lives to save others.

One such incident was at the North Yorkshire coastal town of Whitby, a place surrounded by high hills, cliffs and the looming shadow of the medieval abbey that can be accessed by the famous 199 steps. This is not just a sleepy town, this is where the inspiration for *Dracula* was found and later the wreck of the First World War hospital ship *Rohilla* – a disaster that hit the headlines during the three-day rescue of her occupants.

But on 9 February 1861 there would be both an incredible rescue and a heart-breaking aftermath. Early that morning a storm could be felt blowing throughout the town, and the people sheltering from the wind and rain could only hope that no ships would be out in this, at least not out and in danger. But at around 08:30 it soon became apparent that not only were ships struggling with the huge waves, but they were heading close to shore.

The first launch of the town lifeboat was to the vessel *John and Ann*, struggling in the waves and heading closer to danger with every passing minute. The lifeboat itself needed a crew of around a dozen to handle the craft and pull the survivors on board, but they had successfully rescued all the occupants of the *John and Ann* and returned to shore as heroes. However, the job wasn't over yet.

A schooner named *Gamma* was now aground, forcing the lifeboat crews to reconvene and launch once again to take off the crew. As before, they struggled in the huge waves and spray in their faces as one by one the crew of the *Gamma* were pulled on board and the ship left to her fate.

By now the two rescues had taken their toll on the crew and they brought the boat back exhausted and cold, but it was a good excuse to have a swift glass of grog on their return.

Incredibly, just three hours after their first call, a third ship was now requiring assistance. The *Clara* was grounding close to the previous wreck and so the lifeboat was once again pushed out to rescue the crew. Against all odds, they once again succeeded in bringing the bedraggled crew back to shore. By now they were physically and mentally drained but the sea did not allow them to rest for one minute. Two more ships were in danger.

The *Roe* and the *Utility* were both in serious trouble, and by now word had got out about the heroic rescues the lifeboatmen were undertaking and cheers rang out along the water's edge as the lifeboat headed back out to sea. Amazingly, both ships' crews were brought back in one piece. Five ships' crews were rescued and it was only just early afternoon; the lifeboat crews couldn't take any more. Two other ships nearby were now struggling in the seas, and although the *Flora* managed to navigate into the harbour and tie up away from the storm, the *Merchant* was now in distress. A sixth shipwreck was too much for anybody to have to deal with and the lifeboat crews agreed that they were too exhausted to safely achieve anything.

Memorial to the lifeboatmen lost at Whitby at the nearby Church of St Mary the Virgin. (Author)

Henry Freeman, the only survivor of the Whitby lifeboat disaster. (Frank Sutcliffe, courtesy The Sutcliffe Gallery)

However, as the ship came to grief and the thoughts of stranded sailors played on their minds, humanity got the better of them and each one of them realised that they could not simply stand by and watch their fellow men drown so close to land. The lifeboat was launched once again and thirteen crewmen headed out to what they hoped was the last wreck of this storm.

One of those lifeboatmen was Bridlington-born Henry Freeman, a 25-year-old fisherman who had volunteered to crew the boat just five years earlier when he had moved to the town. What he didn't expect today was what happened when they went out to the *Merchant*.

A huge wave upended the lifeboat and all her crew were thrown into the sea. Already worn down from the five previous rescues, their tired arms could not help them keep their heads above the waves. Each one was thrown around like a toy without a hope of getting back on the upturned lifeboat.

Freeman had a new design of RNLI lifejacket and he had worn it for this mission. His choice had kept him afloat and he struggled ashore as the shocked residents of Whitby witnessed the carnage at sea, helpless to do anything. Who was going to rescue the rescuers?

The other crew members had opted to carry on using the old style of lifejacket, and their choice would cost them their lives. Henry Freeman looked back out to sea and realised that he was the sole survivor. His twelve crewmates were all drowned as the upturned lifeboat drifted on to the shore. Thankfully, the crew of the stricken *Merchant* was rescued later by the use of a rocket line from the shore.

After realising that the one survivor was wearing the new type of lifejacket, the design was soon widely accepted as the better option and was distributed and used accordingly. The inquest into the deaths of the twelve lifeboatmen was opened on

Monday, 11 February by the coroner, John Buchannan Esq., and evidence was heard that highlighted the fact that these men were exhausted to the point of collapse and would struggle to stay alive if they ended up in the water.

The shock of the loss of so many local townsfolk reverberated through the streets. Forty-three children were left without a father and ten women were widowed. The sorrow of the deaths was reflected in the massive turnout at the men's funerals, and even more so at the dedication of the memorial that now stands within St Mary's Church next to the ruins of the abbey. The graves of the heroes of that dreadful day are now weathering and fading as the sea weather that took their lives so long ago threatens to take away their remembrance. The story of the disaster is told with both pride and sorrow at Whitby Lifeboat Museum.

However, this is not where the story ends, as Henry Freeman became one of the most famous lifeboatmen in the country. After the disaster he was awarded a silver medal for bravery and he continued working on the lifeboat. By the time he died in 1904 he had helped save more than 300 lives, and the image of him posing for a photograph with the Whitby life ring is one of the most iconic maritime photos of the time.

By unhappy coincidence, the same thing happened down the coast at Bridlington ten years and one day later. On 10 February 1871, a huge storm drove twenty-eight ships to their doom and capsized the town lifeboat. Six of the crew died as well as dozens of men from the lost ships, but thanks to their efforts the disaster was not as bad as it could have been. In the end, though, like in Whitby, it was just one rescue too many.

Today the Whitby lifeboat station has a modern rescue vessel packed with the latest equipment and lifesaving technology, which includes radios, beacons, a powerful engine and a highly trained crew.

Whitby Lifeboat Museum today. (Author)

Whitby RNLI coxswain Howard Fields, who is in charge of the lifeboat today.
(Whitby Lifeboat)

Howard Fields, the coxswain, has his own his views of how history has helped shape the attitudes of today towards the sea and the respect for their predecessors:

At the time of the 1861 lifeboat disaster in Whitby in which only Henry Freeman survived of the thirteen-man crew, Whitby lifeboat was not then part of the RNLI, which had been established in 1824. Nevertheless, the memory of that fateful day echoes down through history and continues to inspire our lifeboat men of today.

Of course, the training, equipment and lifeboats of today are incomparably better than those of yesteryear when lifeboats were powered by oars. With our 2,860hp MAN diesels, the most up to date navigation and search equipment and capability of 25 knots that can take us over 100 miles from our home base, we provide a lifesaving facility that's the best in the world. But some things haven't changed. The sea is as dangerous as ever and can catch the ill prepared or unwary, and our crews are still mostly volunteers and as ready as in the days of Henry Freeman to risk their lives to save those who are in peril on the sea.

One big change brought about by the 1861 disaster was that Whitby joined the RNLI that same year and has remained a steadfast member ever since.

3

1869: Hosier Lane Family Massacre

At around 08:30 on Monday, 28 June 1869, the police authorities in the Smithfield area of London received a letter from a Mr Walter James Duggen. In it he told them that if they went to a house in the nearby street of Hosier Lane they would find something that would interest them. He also wrote that if they were not let in they should force entry. The street itself had been described as a 'clean, well-kept thoroughfare, at the back of St Sepulchre's Church and immediately in front of one of the main entrances to St Bartholomew's Hospital'.

With this cryptic clue the police had no idea what they might find when they went to investigate, but went around to the house, No. 15. Nobody answered the front door, which was locked on the inside. The two-storey house was somewhat unremarkable, the property of the company next door at No. 16, Messrs Chawner and Co., a silversmith owned by George William Adams, the son-in-law of the original owners. The street itself was named after the fourteenth-century hosiers who lived and worked there to make what today we would call trousers.

When Sergeant Evans could not gain entry to the premises, the police went around the back and managed to get in through a window. What they found upon entry shocked them.

The dead bodies of eight people were in two rooms upstairs that were used as bedrooms. Six of them were children, the two adults assumed to be the parents. In the front bedroom the mother, 40-year-old Emma Duggen, lay on the bed with a child either side of her and another across the foot of the bed, these being Herbert Thomas, aged 4; George Henry, 3; and Ada Frances, 14 months. Another bed in the same room held the bodies of two daughters, Emma, 12, and Jessie, 6. In an adjoining bed was the eldest son, Walter James, 13. In the back room lay the father, 38-year-old Walter, the man who had written the letter to the police. Each of the eight bodies lay in night-clothes in an orderly manner with no evidence of a struggle, a bluish fluid/discoloration on the lips of one or two of them.

What could have caused these people to die? Was it murder? Suicide? It was certainly no accident, that was for sure – which soon became apparent upon the discover of a chair at the side of the mother's bed that had on it a table glass, and a spoon among the bed covers. Bottles of hydrocyanic acid, also known as prussic acid, which was used in the silversmith industry, were found nearby.

The identities of the family members were confirmed by the discovery of a family Bible and the marriage certificate, which gave each person a name and date of birth. Charred paper was found in the kitchen grate but this did not throw any further light on what had gone on in the house.

The neighbours were interviewed and it was noted that the person living opposite had noticed their gas light on between the hours of 03:00 and 04:00 that morning, but this had been turned off by the time the police had arrived at approximately 09:00, just a few hours later. People remarked at how exceedingly fond of his wife Mr Duggen was, and how he had taken the family out for a walk over Blackfriars Bridge that Sunday evening for some fresh air, the house being cramped with so many people living together.

The police called in surgeon Frederick William Wilson from Farringdon Street to give the official notification that all were dead before they could proceed with an investigation. Mr Wilson then had the bodies carried to St Bartholomew's Hospital for post-mortem examinations. With a large number of people now finding out about the house of horrors, bystanders crowded around and were desperate to see something. In those days decorum was just a word that was thrown around; when it came to something like this, everybody wanted to see the action. Some people even approached the police officers with money to allow them access to the crime scene and for a look around the house. All requests were refused.

When police looked into the life of the Duggen family, it was found that Walter had worked for the silversmith for around six or seven years after moving from Bristol. He had lived rent free in the house, which was company owned, and seemed to have a happy life. But recently the family had fallen on hard times when Mr Duggen had grown very ill, and following medical advice he had been forced to leave the company and would soon have to leave the house that came with it.

Walter Duggen's body was identified by his mother, Elizabeth Smith, and she immediately wrote to his brother in Bristol complaining bitterly about his situation and the unkind treatment by his employers, although Mr Adams (his boss) said he could not understand how he could feel this way after the kindness he had shown to the family.

Duggen's state of mind was confirmed the day after when his brother in Bristol came forward with new evidence: a letter, which had been most likely posted at the same time as the police letter. This one went into much greater detail. On the two sides of a sheet of foolscap, Walter spoke about his family affairs and his despair at his current circumstances that led to him giving up his job. He had already given notice and, not having found a new place to live, his notice had expired and he was still living in the house, although his former employers had allowed him a few more days' grace for him to move out in the meantime. He went on to say that the children were poisoned but omitted to mention the person or persons responsible. The wording gave the impression that Duggen had been not only ill but depressed and in absolute despair. He was about to lose everything and end up on the streets with such young children.

By the end of the following day Dr Wilson had carried out post-mortems on four of the bodies and confirmed that the cause of death was poison by prussic acid, the strong odour present during the examination. The smell of it on the mother was so potent that it was apparently 'overpowering'.

Mr Wilson also pointed out that upon examination in situ on the morning of the discovery, rigor mortis had begun to appear in the bodies of the children but not the parents, meaning that the latter had not been dead for long by the time the police had arrived. It was his opinion that the children were most likely fed the poison on a spoon while they lay in bed, and probably while they were sleeping. It was noticeable that the body of the eldest son, Walter James, was slightly turned to one side, as if he had resisted. The body of Walter Senior had been found with both his eyes and mouth open.

The acid bottles found were empty and said to be of the strongest form to be used medicinally. They had only been purchased the Saturday before from a wholesale chemist owned by Mr W. Vorley on 11 King Street, Snow Hill. He had known the buyer simply as 'Fearon' and he signed the purchase book in accordance with the Act of Parliament, although the signature bore a striking resemblance to Walter Duggen's. However, Mr Vorley told the police that the person who purchased the bottles that day was definitely not the deceased.

An inquest heard the evidence from those who examined the bodies and the circumstances that led to the discovery. This is where the letter to Walter Duggen's brother was produced and read out in full:

Frederick Jones Duggan
15, Hosier-lane, Smithfield, E.C,
June 27, 1869.

Dear Brother,
You are aware of Mr. Adam's harsh and bad course of action when he heard my lungs were effected, which ended in his giving me one month's notice to leave his employ, knowing (as I told him) I had no means of livelihood but the one week's wages I left with. His bearing and language have been thoroughly tyrannical from the first moment he heard I was struck down, and have been continued up to the last, and the cause of it all is that he has made a miscalculation in me. He had reckoned he had a good, sound, and serviceable article in me, and when he discovered his mistake he was furious, and showed his annoyance as only a hard, selfish, narrow-minded man could do. After the month expired, he then allowed me after a great deal of solicitation to remain in the house, which is his, a week longer, while I looked for work and a place to live in, which I had no opportunity of doing before. I have tried hard to obtain either or both, but can find no lodging or home, for when they know I am out of work, and can give no reference, they decline altogether. I asked Mr. Adams if he would allow me to name him as a reference. He said he would have nothing to do in the matter, as he might have to pay. I asked him what he thought I could do. He said I could get a place somewhere if I liked, and that I must be out of his house at the expiration of the week, or he would put my things into the lane. I appealed to him for some consideration for my wife and little ones – the eldest he knew was far gone in consumption. I also asked him if it were

possible he could go to such extremes after my being four or five years in his employ, and the long character he had with me, and up to the time of my health partially failing had devoted my whole energy in forwarding his interests. He took no notice of that, but said he would not be trifled with, and unless I was out of his house he would do as he had said, so not to deceive myself in the matter. So, we have to face the alternatives of starving in the streets, the workhouse, or death. We prefer the latter. We may have been able to surmount the possibly [*sic*], if Mr Adams had acted less unfeelingly; but he has shown scant mercy, and if the same is meted to him in his extremity, it will go hard with him, for the blood of me and mine is on his hands, and will cling to him and his. It is better to meet death as we have than to wait till he comes through want, privation, and misery, and would come with equal certainty for me, Emma, and all the children are far from strong, and must have quickly succumbed. We are strongly attached to each other, and separation alone would be as bad as death, and we love the children dearly – too dearly to condemn them to utter wretchedness and want. It is agony of mind almost beyond endurance to think that the alternative is so terrible that we cannot shield it from one or the other. Break the news gently to mother. Tell her it is, under the circumstances, the best course – far better than the degradation and want and disease before us, which must have ended in the same way after all our sufferings. Prussic acid was the thing used. Pray undertake the funerals if you can. I trust you will have enough things to pay expenses. Oh! the horror of this night. May it be visited upon the man who forced it! I can write no more. I am nearly mad. So an eternal farewell to you all, and may God bless you! Farewell forever!

Duggen's employer, Mr Adams, stood up to give evidence, confirming that he was the owner of numbers 13 to 18 Hosier Lane and that the deceased had been in his employment. He had given notice to leave on 3 April 1869 due to Mr Duggen's ill health. At first he thought it was just a cold but it seemed he had issues with his lungs, suggesting consumption (tuberculosis). Although Mr Adams claimed that he tried to change his mind, Duggen was adamant that he could not continue any further with his employment and feared that he would not get any better. A visit to Bristol led to nothing that would help him find work. Mr Adams said he spoke to Mr Duggen on Thursday, 24 June, and said that his house must be vacated, although when Duggen told him that he still had not found work or accommodation, Adams agreed to extend his stay until midday on Monday, which, Mr Adams claimed, Duggen did not even thank him for.

Explaining that he was not a harsh man, Adams informed the hearing that he had never been asked for a reference and if he had been he would not have refused one. Normal notice was a week but he had given Duggen two months. More to the point, Adams did not use prussic acid and had no use for it.

A jury did not take long in giving their verdict, 'That Walter James and Emma Duggen murdered their six children, and afterwards destroyed their own lives, whilst in an unsound state of mind.'

The building itself at 15 Hosier Lane was later the premises of the new oil merchant and refiner Phoenix Supply Co., which was established there in 1890, specialising in engineers' tools, rubber hoses, oils, lubricants and balata beltings. Over time the discovery of the bodies was forgotten about; with so many major events coming and going, the newspapers reported for a few days and then never again graced their pages with the Duggen family.

London suffered under the attacks by Luftwaffe bombers during the Second World War and photographs taken by the RAF after the war showed half of Hosier Lane no longer there. Today the site of the murders is a modern office building, with nothing to show the people walking past what horrors greeted the police over a century and half ago, when depression and despair led to mass murder and suicide.

All details published in newspaper reports from the time of the incident and in the few days after.

4

1893: Sinking of SS *Gwendoline*

Many ships have vanished over the centuries; some are never written about again, and will remain forgotten until someday a long-forgotten scrap of information is read and the disappearance can be reinvestigated. The vessels and their crews were once the forefront of conversation: the shiny new ship being launched, and the men saying farewell to their loved ones on the dock side never to be seen again. One of these lost ships is the SS *Gwendoline*.

It was through my love of shipwrecks that I first heard about the *Gwendoline* from a colleague, Andy Brighty, who had been doing some family history research. He had traced his family back several generations and thought I should hear about his discovery. He found that his great-great-grandfather, Thomas Aiston, was a donkeyman on board and had been lost at sea.

A donkeyman was an engineer who worked down in the bowels of the ship on the engines, particularly the 'donkey engine', which was a steam-powered winch used to raise and lower sails, and hoist cargo via winches or power pumps, hence the donkey work.

This knowledge led me to dig a bit deeper into the history of the ship and once again I came across yet another forgotten disaster.

Built as SS *Redcar* at Sir Raylton Dixon & Co. in Middlesbrough and launched on 8 June 1876, her name was changed immediately to the *Gwendoline*. She was a collier of 525 gross tons and 164ft long, but could take other cargoes too. The single-screw steamer usually had a crew of around twelve plus her captain on the journeys up and down the east coast of the United Kingdom. Her owners, the Swan Brothers of Middlesbrough, were led by Herbert Arthur Swan. Although she was a steamship, she was also rigged as a schooner, fitted with deck pumps as well as those fitted in connection with her engines.

She was swung for compass adjustments in the Tees Bay on 23 June 1880, with some slight corrections made. On 31 January 1881 she was cleared to proceed to sea from Middlesbrough, bound for Grangemouth with 650 tons of pig iron. She had been under the command of Thomas Smith since the previous August and carried a crew of fourteen, including Smith, on this voyage. The weather was good until the ship arrived off St Abb's Head early the following morning, when it started to become foggy. The ship was slowed down and bearings taken as best as could be done, as well as soundings. The ship stopped in the water and a boat came close with two men in. When they were hailed, they revealed the ship was between Battery Point and Inch Garvie, neither of which could be seen at this point.

With the crew not realising just how close they were to land, the ship slowly made its way north-west when suddenly the top of Inch Garvie was seen close by and the engines were immediately put full speed astern, the help on hard-a-port. However, it was too late: the ship struck the rocks aft and lost two blades from her propeller, and water began coming into the ship.

The captain ordered the engines stopped and the steam pumps began working to repel the water that was flooding the damaged aft section of the ship, which was located at the collision bulkhead. As the ship began filling with water, Captain Smith made the decision to beach her, running her aground just to the north-west of Port Edgar.

The ship was saved, for now, and over the next few weeks the cargo was taken off and the *Gwendoline* was refloated on 19 February with the assistance of tugs, which towed the damaged vessel into Grangemouth for repairs. A court of inquiry just weeks later heard evidence of the circumstances that led to the grounding and found that the captain should not have attempted to navigate through fog via the narrows of the Queensferry Channel. Instead, he should have gone to anchor and waited until the fog cleared before proceeding. Familiarity with the channel, it was said, made the captain overconfident to the point that he thought that he could navigate through in the bad conditions and arrive on time. On 4 March 1881, the court suspended Captain Smith's master's certificate for three months and put the grounding down to 'negligence in the navigating of his ship, causing her thereby to sustain material damage'.

The years went by and the *Gwendoline* continued to be of service to her owners, many a crew member joining and leaving – one of thousands of iron-hulled vessels now ploughing through the North Sea on their journeys, many of which had a chequered history.

On Friday, 17 November 1893, at around 20:00, the *Gwendoline* was loaded with her cargo of coal in Borrowstounness (also known as Bo'ness) on the south bank of the Firth of Forth, Scotland. She was under the command of 40-year-old Captain John Mallet, who lived on Wentworth Terrace in Middlesbrough with his wife Annie and 16-year-old son Conrad.

The First Mate, Thomas Miller of Falkirk, who was married, had previously been a master for the Carron Line, running between Grangemouth and London, and had recently left the steamer *Abergrange* to join the *Gwendoline*.

The other crew members at the time were Second Mate Sown; Lamp Trimmer Christenson; Steward John Allan of Grangemouth, who was married; Seaman Jonathon Coombs of Middlesbrough; Seaman Jacklin; Seaman Campaign; Chief Engineer Henry Pringle, from Saltburn; Second Engineer Wright; Fireman T. Scott of 51 Snowdon Road, Middlesbrough; Fireman Edwards; and, of course, Donkeyman Thomas Aiston of Gladstone Street, who had replaced the usual donkeyman, Amos, sent home after a death in the family.

The *Gwendoline* was bound for the port of Hull, at the southernmost end of the East Yorkshire coast, and then into the River Humber, a journey that was regular for ships of this class. Slipping her lines and proceeding out to sea up the Firth of Forth, it was not long before she had cleared the river and had turned towards her destination. Her arrival in Hull was set for the afternoon of Sunday, 19 November, as long as the upcoming choppy seas did not delay her too much.

However, the ship was never seen again. The port noted that her arrival was late but there was no word on where she was or if there was a delay due to the weather being stormy along her route. Ships did have a habit of running late, especially when the seas picked up, but now this was not just a few hours, this was turning into days.

Wreckage was located in the middle of the following week off the coast of Flamborough Head, and even more was found in the coming days off Holy Island further north. One of the pieces was a lifebelt bearing the name *Gwendoline*. Now it became apparent that the ship had been lost with all hands soon after setting sail. This was confirmed on 22 November, when a body was located and soon identified as that of her captain, John Mallet.

By Friday, 24 November, the coroner for Northumberland, Charles Percy, held an inquest at the Castle Inn at Seahouses, a small harbour close to where the *Gwendoline* was thought to have gone down. A shipping agent for the area, Mr Hodgson, confirmed the identity of the body as that of the captain and he told the coroner the details relating to the loss of the ship as well as the general statistics of the 17-year-old steamer. He had also identified some of the wreckage as being from the lost ship and he stated that, in his opinion, the *Gwendoline* had been sunk in the gale not far from where they now stood. The jury returned a verdict of drowning due to the loss of his ship 'in the neighbourhood of the Farne Islands'. The coroner ended the inquest by thanking those involved in helping with this sad duty, particularly coastguard Mr Collis and local police officer Sergeant Brown.

The body of Captain Mallet was buried in Linthorpe Cemetery near to another body later recovered, that of Robert Wright, aged 29. Their stories are told by a local history society, the Friends of Linthorpe Cemetery and Nature Reserve, which researches the graves and the people interred there.

The wreck of the *Gwendoline* was later located off the coast of St Abb's Head at a depth of between 213 and 232ft pointing at 120 degrees on a sandy seabed. Divers report that the ship is well broken up after over a century on the sea floor, the timber structure now fallen away revealing her coal still in the holds. A compass has been found decaying but still intact, as well as a large serving platter with a picture of a swan in the centre for Swan Brothers, her owners.

With her depth being out of reach for sport divers, her visits are few and far between, allowing her and the lost crew to rest in peace, forever a part of history that is now no longer forgotten.

5

1907: Sowerby Bridge Tram

The tram was a popular and necessary mode of transport in the early twentieth century, and it is still popular today with both enthusiasts and big city networks. Part bus, part train, trams are run on railway lines within the main roads and fed by electricity via overhead cables down a connection called a trolley pole, to give them the power needed. The main safety issue has always been the fact that trams have to share the roads with cars, bicycles and people and they cannot turn and move out of the way – only go forward, backwards and stop. It is therefore up to all other moving objects to get out of the way to prevent an accident.

One particular tram route run by the Halifax Corporation was through the market town of Sowerby Bridge in West Yorkshire, a small place consisting of a group of shops, a church and two schools in the Upper Calder Valley. All the roads going to and from the nearby towns have steep inclines and it is one of those places that is quiet yet busy. Bolton Brow is one of the main roads running through it, and is the primary access out of the town and towards Halifax and the neighbouring cities of Leeds and Bradford.

Bolton Brow tram. (Calderdale Libraries)

On Tuesday, 15 October 1907, the country awoke to the news that a rail crash in Shrewsbury had killed more than a dozen people with the death toll still rising, but few people had even heard about this as they boarded the early morning tram, the No. 64, for work that morning and found a seat for the short ride through Sowerby Bridge. This route had been the scene of a near disaster a year ago when a tram car slipped backwards on the hill and inadvertently cut the power, sending it rolling down the road. The car killed a horse and injured eight people, who were forced to jump for their lives as it hurtled towards disaster. Thankfully, this seemed to be a one-off: a freak accident that should not happen again. Now an array of alternative braking systems gave the driver at least three ways to bring a tram to a halt – a much-needed fallback that was especially needed here.

Tram 64 was a 7½-ton car consisting of two decks and two 35hp motors powered on four wheels. The brakes were of three different kinds – a mechanical slipper brake on both rails, wheel brakes applied by hand, and a rheostatic electric brake with Westinghouse type-90 controllers.

After the last accident, the drivers had raised the issue of the current leading to the tram car cutting out in places, not much but enough to leave the car without enough power to be controlled. At around 05:50 on that dark and foggy morning, the passengers were ten minutes into their journeys. The seats were wet and this made for an unpleasant experience sitting down, but as the tram headed up Bolton Brow and almost cleared the peak, the lights suddenly went out both inside and out and the car came to a stop. Instead of going forwards, the tram was felt to be rolling backwards back down the hill they had just come up.

The driver, Thomas Simpson, tried to apply the brakes but the wet cables had very little grip with the momentum of a heavy car pushing against them. The tram had to navigate around two curves in the road, which incredibly it did, staying upright, but now it was going at full speed, much to the horror of its occupants. Some took

HALIFAX TRAM ACCIDENT AT SOWERBY BRIDGE, Oct. 15th, 1907.

Bolton Brow tram. (Calderdale Libraries)

a chance and jumped off the out-of-control vehicle, not knowing if they were going to live or die. One of them was seen to tumble into the road but, by some miracle, was not seriously hurt. By now the tram car had picked up considerable speed and was a death trap waiting to come to a crashing stop. The trolley pole was caught up and torn clear of the roof and, with an increased momentum that left the terrified passengers fearing for their lives, the tram finally left the tracks and struck the sides of nearby buildings, the speed not decreasing the entire time, before its left side slammed on to the road and scraped to a halt after around 250yd of sheer terror.

The noise of the crash woke the nearby residents, who looked out of their windows and doors in horror at what they were seeing. The injured occupants emerged dazed and confused, the conductor, 35-year-old Walter Robinson, lying among the most badly injured. He had stuck to his post the entire time and prevented people from leaping off to certain death. Now he was himself dead within the wreckage, near the body of a passenger who had been flung from the car when it finally flipped over. The top deck was completely ripped off and lay close by. The main body of the tram was at a crazy angle, pointing towards the side street East Parade, debris strewn all across the cobbled road.

Locals raced to the scene to see if they could help the injured, and a telephone alert was sent out for ambulances to come as quickly as possible. The St John Ambulance Brigade and local doctors from all over the town dropped what they were doing or were woken up to head straight to the crash site in order to administer first aid. More than two dozen people were now needing medical attention, some with serious wounds that required them to be rushed to hospital, although some would not make it through the day. The nearby Shepherds Rest pub, just yards away from where the tram came to rest, was used as a temporary casualty handling station to get the injured out of the cold and into the light. One by one those injured were transferred by ambulance carriages to

Halifax Infirmary, where doctors worked on the more seriously wounded. Incredibly, the driver, who had heroically stuck to his post while trying to stop the car, was not injured. Those now lying in hospital beds had fractured bones, concussion, a broken nose and various cuts and bruises.

Some victims had to be recovered from underneath the tram and it was lifted slightly in order to achieve this. There was no shortage of volunteers, and it seemed as if hundreds, even thousands, of people had turned up to help. Nearby homes opened their doors to the injured and allowed them inside for comfort and to recover from the shock or to have their wounds treated. Some were considered well enough to actually go straight home, although the trauma of what had happened would have naturally stayed with them despite the absence of physical injuries and broken bones.

By the end of the day, four people had been confirmed dead, with thirty-seven others injured. The second rail crash in just a few hours made for grim reading in the newspapers. For the investigators, an inquest had already been opened into the deaths and serious questions were being asked as to how power could be lost at such a critical moment of a tram ascending a hill.

The Board of Trade launched an inquiry led by Lieutenant Colonel E. Druitt, RE, who took it upon himself to visit the scene of the crash as word came through that a fifth person had died of his injuries five days after the disaster. It was heard that the route up to the top of Bolton Brow at Pye Nest was lethal and that driver Simpson was one of the best in the business.

On 23 October an inquest at the Sowerby Bridge Council offices into the deaths of the victims ended with the jury returning a unanimous opinion that the management were to blame for the disaster and recommended that a tram going up such a steep incline should have no fewer than three staff on board, one driver and two conductors. Despite their misgivings, they returned a verdict of accidental death on the first three victims. A second inquest into the deaths of the two other passengers was held, with the same witnesses being called to give evidence. They returned the same verdict, with the recommendation that the tram controllers and brakes should be all alike and that there should be a man at the rear platform to operate such devices. The driver admitted that he had failed to notice the style of controller on this tram and that his actions could have led to the slowing down of the car rather than it speeding up, but his initial thinking and actions towards a different type of controller had led to him believing that there was no way to slow the tram from its descent.

The Tramway Committee implemented these changes immediately, and incredibly the same thing happened yet again at the exact same place. The current went off, leaving the tram rolling backwards, but the extra operators on board prevented a disaster and stopped the car. This was not before several passengers had jumped off the runaway tram but thankfully nobody was injured. The incident proved that the alterations were both needed and lifesaving, and had been implemnted without a delay.

As the years went by the tram accident was forgotten. There is no plaque to commemorate what happened at the site but a local historian did publish a small booklet with images and information from the *Halifax Guardian*. What is shocking is not that there were so many near misses on this hill, but that another disaster occurred within a few metres of the tram crash eighty-six years later in a horrifyingly similar accident, but with a different type of vehicle.

Bolton Brow had not changed that much. The trams had long gone, along with the cobbled road, replaced by tarmac and traffic lights as the modern day dawned on this small town. On Monday, 6 September 1993, the children of Sowerby Bridge were heading to school for the day and a British Telecom van was making its way around a roundabout, the nearby shops opening for another day's business. Suddenly, a lorry came speeding over the hill and slammed into the BT van, mounted the kerb and ploughed into the front of the post office sending bricks, masonry and wreckage in all directions.

As the dust cloud billowed up into the air, the realisation of what had happened sunk in. The houses and post office were destroyed, the BT van was flattened underneath the truck and even worse was the fact that a young woman and her daughter were last seen stood in front of the shop. It later transpired that the disaster could have been much worse as just moments before the crash the shop had been full of children, but they had just left. But this did not soften the blow when it was revealed that six people had been killed.

That day was one that the emergency services will never forget as they had to bring heavy lifting gear to haul the wreckage clear and recover the bodies, while at the same time be mindful of the fact that the building was on the verge of collapse all around them. When the investigation was complete, the owners of the lorry were fined £5,000 by magistrates after they admitted to using a heavy goods vehicle with defective brakes. The victims included the driver of both the truck and the van, two occupants of the shop, and the mother and 2-year-old girl stood outside.

What is incredible is that this hill had been known as a road accident black spot for a long time, with cars and vans constantly going above the speed limit and causing concern for the local residents. Traffic-calming methods had slowed them down but this did not stop the out-of-control lorry from causing death and destruction within seconds.

Today the area is once again back to normal, the Shepherds Rest pub is still there on the corner and the shop where the lorry crashed was demolished to make way for a memorial garden to the six who died in the 1993 disaster. It is inevitable that so many near tragedies had occurred there before two major ones were to take a total of eleven lives almost nine decades apart. It seems that history tends to repeat itself if lessons are not learned. This would not be the first time two disasters, decades apart, have occurred at the exact same spot (see 1925: Dibbles Bridge).

In Sowerby Bridge people will always remember those lost in the modern crash, while history enthusiasts will seem to be the only ones who will know about the tram. With the story now told here, heroes such as conductor Walter Robinson will be forever remembered by those who read about his brave action that cost him his life.

6

1908: Barnsley Public Hall Crush

There are many disasters that fill the reader with horror, but none are more shocking than those which involve the deaths of a large number of children. In 1966 a coal tip slid off the side of a mountain in the Welsh village of Aberfan and went straight over the top of a school. A total of 144 people were killed including 116 children, making this one of the most shocking disasters of the twentieth century. Further back, the liner *City of Benares* was sunk while taking evacuees across the Atlantic and seventy-seven children were drowned. In 1996 a mass shooting at Dunblane Primary School left sixteen children and their teacher dead.

In 1908 there was another disaster that made headlines but few people outside of the immediate area have heard of it. It happened at the public hall in the centre of the South Yorkshire town of Barnsley.

Built by Henry Harvey in 1877, the hall was intended to allow the local working-class residents of the town access to education and training, with the emphasis on aspects of social bettering and enlightenment of the mind. The School of Art made its home there in 1878 and it was the place to be for those who sought knowledge. The hall was officially handed over

A locally produced commemorative postcard of the disaster. (Reproduced with kind permission of Barnsley Archives and Local Studies)

to the Corporation in 1890 by Charles Harvey and structural alterations were carried out, which included adding a staircase to the galley. This would later have an iron rail installed following an inspection by West Riding County Council after the hall was licensed to stage plays in September 1892. From that point the staircase satisfied all inspections.

On Saturday, 11 January 1908, the World's Cinematograph Company had rented the hall for a number of viewings of films at a special low price of just one penny. It soon became apparent that one of the galleys was overcrowded, with estimates later putting the number of people in this area at more than 1,000, although there were only enough seats for 400. Therefore it was decided to move the children in this room to a better spot on the lower level, and so they were ushered out of the galley and directed down the stairs into the lower part known as 'the pit'.

Many of the children realised that there was a chance they could get a good viewing place so they took off down the stairs like rockets. They wanted to hurry as the performance was due to start soon, at around 14:00 to 14:30. People were still queuing to get in but they had to be turned away due to the number of people inside.

At this point a large number of children were racing *up* the stairs, eager to get seats in the places that were already overcrowded. They met the stampede of children coming in the opposite direction and this led to several falling over on the stairs. It is estimated that around 200 of these children were on the staircase alone, and within seconds there was pandemonium.

A ticket collector shouted to the caretaker that children were falling down the stairs and this was causing a crush of people now falling on top of each other at the bottom. With that many people now falling, there were dozens trapped tightly together and screaming for help, unable to breathe and being crushed with so many bodies on top that they could not push them off. The caretaker, George Burkinshaw, was first to give a hand and raced to pull children out of the pile and get them out of the way. However, this was fast turning into a major incident that the few staff could not handle. The suddenness of the crush led to a lot of children screaming to get out as they were pushed up against the staircase wall, the stairs and other people pressed against them.

With a general panic threatening to make the situation even worse, the first picture was put on for the people in the galley so that they would stay put and not come out and cause an even bigger disaster. That way they would be oblivious to what was going on and hopefully the problem would be cleared by the time the picture finished. The screening was started and the hundreds of children were none the wiser.

The local police station was telephoned and several officers raced to the scene, nearby shops seeing the drama and their owners and workers rushing to help. Children were pulled out of the pile as quickly as possible and the entire incident was over in just ten minutes. However, there were sixteen children lying dead, laid out on straw in the yard at the foot of the galley staircase.

Alberta Fairhurst was 8 years old and one of the girls who had arrived that day with a friend to watch the entertainment, only to find herself right in the middle of the chaos. She was pulled out of the pile of bodies, still clutching her entrance fee. Her friend was not so lucky and was among those who died. Alberta would only mention this incident to her family on the odd occasion during her life, as her sadness prevented her from talking about it much. Even when she passed away in 1978, her family would always remember her telling this terrible and shocking story.

Beckett Hospital had a sudden influx of children with injuries – some estimated that up to forty were suffering from some kind of bodily injury or trauma – but despite the large number that had been in the crush, only seven were actually detained in hospital, while another twenty were treated for smaller injuries and discharged straight away. Within a few days there were only three still in hospital.

Once the stairs had been cleared it was necessary to stop the performance and those inside were told that there had been an accident outside the galley and that the show would not be continuing today. They quietly, quickly and in an orderly manner filed out of the building and went home.

The inquest took place at Barnsley Town Hall and was opened on Monday, 13 January, by the coroner J.P. Maitland. He agreed to allow only the evidence of identification to be given so that the funerals could go ahead. Many of the parents giving evidence were in tears. A double tragedy had struck the family of victim John Charles Graham that very day, when the boy's father died from heart disease brought on by the stress of the sudden death of his son. His wife Lily Graham was called before the inquest and, in floods of tears, announced that her husband was now also dead; the coroner didn't keep her a moment longer than necessary and apologised for her being called to appear.

The medical evidence revealed that all the deaths were due to suffocation. The coroner questioned if the number of tickets issued were one cause, after their free distribution to children in schools as flyers for the event. It was found that the people in the building to control the guests were thin on the ground: just a few ticket collectors taking the money as they arrived in the seating areas themselves, the caretaker and twelve performers that came with the entertainment company. This number, plus a few workmen present on the day, led to the jury finding that the children died because of the lack of staff provided, which led to bad regulation of the children around the staircase, but this was not, in this case criminal negligence. The coroner went on to say that the integrity and safety of the staircase itself was not under any doubt. He ended the inquest on 17 January by paying tribute to those who had saved lives that day, both at the public hall and at the hospital.

The funerals took place all that week and were not a mass gathering. Instead there were separate memorials for each child, the Mayor sending a wreath to be placed on each coffin. The King and the Prince of Wales later sent their condolences to the Mayor of Barnsley, Councillor J.S. Rose, and he then took it around to each individual home that had lost someone. It was reported that most of the children were insured and therefore the funerals were paid for. The Mayor attended as many as he could in person while receiving condolences from across the country.

Barnsley Public Hall was later used as headquarters during the First World War for the Barnsley Pals, 'pals' being the collective name for groups of locals across the country who signed up together and took on the name of their home town before going off to fight in the trenches. In 1962 it was revamped and renamed Barnsley Civic Theatre until it closed to the public in 1998.

On 11 January 2008 a memorial ceremony took place there, attended by locals, a relative of two of the victims and the current Mayor Len Picken, who then unveiled a plaque that named all sixteen victims, all of them between the ages of 4 and 8. Engraved on it was an extract from a memorial card printed at the time that simply read, 'Little they thought their time so short in this world to remain.'

However, that was not the end of the story for the building itself. A group of enthusiasts worked hard on preserving the history and successfully renamed the building The Civic. They reopened it in 2009 as a theatre and art gallery, although many of the original features remained out of bounds until it could be restored back to its former glory, which they hoped to do over time. During redevelopment the staircase where the disaster happened was demolished and now only the plaque is there to remind us what happened However, with the building now open once again, the young victims will be remembered beyond just a bunch of scattered headstones in a graveyard.

7

1925: Dibbles Bridge Coach Crash (1)

Road accidents in Britain are quite common and ever since the motor vehicle was invented people have become victims of the collisions, mishaps and scrapes that followed the developments of cars as they became bigger, better and faster. With the introduction of the bus, vast numbers of people could make short journeys without having the expense of owning a car or the responsibility of having to navigate the roads in all kinds of weather. Needless to say, whenever a new type of vehicle was introduced, accidents occurred and so did the deaths of the people on board. One of these places was Dibbles Bridge in the North Yorkshire countryside.

A legend has it that one day a shoemaker to the monks of Fountains Abbey saw that the river was a raging torrent. As he struggled to cross, he saw an image of the devil himself and shared with him his eel pie and sack, for which the devil thanked him by having a bridge put over the river. From then on it was known as Devil's Bridge, although this was rebuilt in the 1600s. Depending on what you believe, it is most likely a play on words, with 'dibble' sounding a bit like 'devil'. But it would soon be known once again as Devil's Bridge after a terrible tragedy cemented its place in local history.

On Wednesday, 10 June 1925, a party of sixty members of the York Municipal Employees Guild along with some of their relatives were taking a trip up to Wharfedale for their annual outing. They were split into three groups and each group was given an open-top bus known as a charabanc for their journey.

These stylish coaches were known as Maudesleys, and were owned by local company Whitby C. Oliver & Son. They normally had furniture built into the body but had had seats fitted just five days before for the start of the holiday season so they could carry passengers. Should it rain, a light canvas cover could be rigged up to keep the people on board dry. The convoy of coaches set off at around 08:30 that morning for what it was hoped would be an exciting day out in the Yorkshire countryside, an opportunity to get some fresh air away from the bustle of the city and thoughts of work. The itinerary included visits to Burnsall, Barden Tower, Bolton Abbey and Ilkley, which would turn out to be an excellent day if the sunshine and heat continued.

All was well until 13:00, when the three coaches were transiting the road between Pateley Bridge and the village of Grassington, heading westbound through a very green area with fields for miles around and often no sign of civilisation other than the odd farmhouse dotted around and occasional passing traffic. The roads themselves are long and winding, the hills creeping up on the coaches both ascending and descending. It was on a brow of the road known as Fancarl Hill that the last coach in the convoy, with twenty-three passengers on board, developed problems.

Driver William Elsegood had a good safety record, with around eight years' experience. He stopped the coach at the top of the next hill for adjustments to be made to the machinery underneath and, satisfied that the coach was OK, carried on the journey, the other two coaches now well ahead and out of sight. However, as the vehicle gathered speed it was soon apparent that it was going faster than it should be as the weight of the coach on the steep

Dibbles Bridge coach crash, 1925.

road helped it gather momentum. Mr Elsegood now realised that the brakes he had just checked had failed, and despite attempts to keep the coach on a slow downward run he was now unable to control it. All he could do now was try his hardest to turn on the bend at the bottom of the hill and attempt to keep the coach on the road. Knowing that there was nothing he could do, he simply announced, 'She's going!'

The coach just kept getting faster, although the passengers were surprisingly calm, probably stunned at what they were seeing. One of the passengers, Mr Hartley, made a leap for it and landed with only minor injuries, but he could only watch in horror as the coach struck the bridge over the River Dibb on the right-hand side, causing the vehicle to skid across the road and plough through the stone parapet. Then, to the jumper's horror, it plunged over the side of the bridge into the void below.

The coach came to rest upside down after a 36ft drop from the road. The parapet was completely gone where the coach had smashed through it, its stones following the vehicle down. The passengers were now trapped under the wreckage, seven of them dead or dying and the rest seriously injured. The sound of groaning from those too dazed and battered to be able to help themselves rung out from the mess. Mr Hartley had chased the bus towards its final resting place and looked in horror at the sight that now greeted him. The front of the bus was pointing towards the direction of travel, its radiator lying loose. The wheels were pointing skywards at a crazy angle, with the rear end hanging over the edge of the grass and pointing down into the river below. The body of the bus was on top of a 4ft-high wall that separated the land from the water, this possibly stopping the wreckage from sliding down into the stream and causing further casualties.

The place where they now stood was Dibbles Bridge, a notorious accident black spot that had seen previous collisions caused by vehicles' failure to slow down enough at the bend. This, though, had been by far the most serious incident, and now seventeen people needed medical attention in what seemed like the middle of nowhere. Incredibly, the driver survived, pinned down in his seat. He struggled to pull himself out and staggered to the embankment in a state of shock.

Harry Cardus was a farmer living at Laburnum Farm in the small village of Appletreewick. Thirty-three years old, he would regularly head out on horseback to tend to his sheep and cattle in the surrounding rolling countryside, and was working near the crash site at the time. When somebody came and informed him that there had been a bad accident at the bridge, he headed over there straight away to see if he could help. By the time he got there it was obvious that there was very little he could do, those injured now being tended to and another local, haulier Herbert Longthorn, was also helping out where he could. The injured were suffering from both their injuries from the crash and the heat from the sun beating down on them. Many were in very uncomfortable positions. Improvised stretchers were being used to bring the survivors back to the road, one being the nearby gate that was taken off its hinges.

Eventually word hadspread and emergency teams arrived to extract the survivors and take them up to the main road and on to waiting vehicles. The injured were taken away to Skipton District Hospital, and thankfully the death toll did not rise any further. Due to the lack of communication between the coaches, the other two parties did not know about the fate of the others until they returned back to Exhibition Square later that day, when they were greeted by a crowd of people wondering if their relatives were alive or dead. The Lord Mayor of York, Sir Robert Newbald Kay, had already made the journey to the site of the crash that evening to see the devastation for himself and to visit the injured in hospital. Together with Stanley Slack, the Sheriff of York, they spoke to the doctors and nurses and expressed their gratitude at the incredible work they had done for the survivors. Just twenty-four hours after the disaster most people were being discharged from hospital, and this included the driver.

On the day after the crash, an inquest was opened at Grassington Sanatorium by coroner Edgar Wood and, after taking only evidence of identification of the seven victims, it was adjourned until the end of the month. On 30 June 1925 it was resumed at Grassington Town Hall, with evidence being heard from the doctor on the scene from the Bradford Corporation Sanatorium, who gave details of the injuries he saw that day. It was revealed that all those killed were in the second and third rows of seats, and this coincided with the fact that those seats hit a dry-stone wall as the coach landed upside down. The owners of the coach stated the vehicle was in a good condition, having been overhauled just the month before, this being only its second trip since then. An engineer from Leeds gave evidence to say that when he examined the wreckage, although the working parts were in good condition, the brake drums were in fact rather oily. This would have reduced the ability to slow the vehicle and was, in his opinion, the primary cause of the disaster.

The jury took just twenty minutes to return a verdict of accidental death and added, 'We hold no one guilty of culpable negligence.' Their verdict came with two other recommendations. Firstly, that a sign be put up at the top of the hill to state that 'This hill is dangerous and all drivers of heavy vehicles must change to low gear and advise passengers to walk down'. Secondly, they stated that the bridge should be widened and that the previous accident there should have served as a warning that this needed to be done, and that those responsible for doing the alterations should not have waited until people were lying dead before carrying out action.

The victims of the crash were taken back to York and the funerals carried out, with a memorial service held at York Minster on 15 June. The seven victims were interred in York and Fulford cemeteries. Over time the disaster at Dibbles Bridge would be forgotten, just like so many others.

That remained the case until a few days before the crash's fiftieth anniversary, when the son of farmer Harry Cardus would see history repeat itself once again.

8

1927: Hull Rail Disaster

The city of Hull on the East Yorkshire coast has been at the forefront of the fishing industry for many a year, and as the city grew the need for a reliable railway line grew with it. The train platforms built at Hull Paragon made up the terminal station, the trains that arrived and departed here coming from all the major lines such as Scarborough via Bridlington, Sheffield via Doncaster, Leeds, and as far away as London.

One of the lines that no longer exists led to Withernsea. On 14 February 1927 a nine-carriage train from here was heading towards Hull driven by Robert Dixon. Meanwhile, the 09:05 service was leaving Hull bound for Scarborough, departing with six carriages and now slowly heading out on the northbound journey under the control of driver Samuel Atkinson, a man with almost three decades of experience. The numerous tracks outside Hull Paragon ran in a westward direction before each one branched out towards their respective onward stations west and north. The two trains should have passed each other around this point without a problem, as they had done so many times before. But today there was a slight problem that would quickly turn catastrophic for the Hull railway.

Hull Paragon rail crash. (Courtesy Steve Bramley)

As the outbound train ran under the signal gantry at Park Street, and still within sight of the station, Atkinson had the strange feeling that his train had been switched on to the wrong track. He checked on both sides of the footplate and, once he was certain that this was so, he slammed on his brakes and brought his train to a halt, although it may still have been moving very slowly. However, by this time it was already too late – at 09:10 the Scarborough train was right in the path of the inbound train from Withernsea and with just seconds left, and with the two trains closing at no more than 16mph, both drivers braced for a collision. The Withernsea train would not have known that another train was on the line until it was too late, such is the layout of the track in this area. By the time both drivers realised and applied the brakes it would have slowed them by probably 1mph but nothing more. When they were closer than one carriage length away, Fireman Charles

Wilkinson shouted, 'Look out!' to Driver Atkinson as they both helplessly watched disaster coming in straight ahead.

The trains crashed head on, the two engines ripping into each other and telescoping into the carriages. Wooden structures and metal framework split and flew in every direction as passengers were jolted forward and thrown to the front of their seating. As the wreckage settled and the dazed and injured passengers realised what had just happened, the railway line was in a shocking state. The tender of the outbound Scarborough train was now under the roof of the front half of the Withernsea train's lead coach, the first five compartments crushed into each other and trapping dozens of passengers, many of whom were families on a day out. It was only the last four coaches of the Withernsea train that were undamaged.

By extraordinary luck, the crash had happened at the Argyle Street Bridge right next to Hull Institution Hospital (where the modern Hull Royal Infirmary is today), which gave a fighting chance to anybody who was too badly injured to journey any further. The local residents who started to descend on the scene had only witnessed the horrors of the First World War less than a decade ago, but even so, they were left in shock at the carnage laid out before them. The trains were fitted with gas lights on board and it was only a miracle that these did not cause more destruction by exploding (as was the case in 1915 at Quintinshill, Britain's worst rail crash).

But as the clouds of dirt and steam began to dissipate, those left alive were faced by a horrific sight. The bodies of several passengers were hanging from the upper carriage sections, limbs hanging loose, and the smashing of the wood and glass fragments left many victims with injuries so bad that they would not survive for much longer.

Driver Sam Atkinson found himself in the coal storage, flung there by the force of the collision, but still alive and able to move. When he had gathered his head together he jumped down and ran up to the steps of the nearby signal box to find out what had happened.

By now people were being dragged out of the train carriages by anybody in the area who could help. The cries of those trapped within the wreckage were being heard but the doctors, nurses, locals and railway staff could only get to them one at a time. The twisted wood and metal structures were a nightmare to try to work around and they didn't want to cause the victims more injury than necessary in their attempts to free them.

Nurses from the infirmary at the Anlaby Road Poor Law Institution scrambled over the fencing on ladders to reach the accident site. Holes were made in the fence to allow ease of access and for the injured to be taken away without having to hoist them over a great height, which would have caused even more distress to people who were already only just clinging on to life.

The fireman on the Withernsea train, Thomas Scott, was praised by passengers after he 'plunged into the work of rescuing the dead and injured', blood pouring from cuts to his face, and another man was seen holding up a piece of wreckage to allow access to the injured, despite 'blood flowing freely' from his leg. At the time it was reported that, 'He steadfastly refused to leave his task in order to have his own wounds dressed'.

In the meantime, the other railway tracks remained open and a service was still operating in and out of Hull. A train bound for Liverpool went past and the passengers were shocked at the horrors that they could not only see with their own eyes, but also hear the screams of the injured, bringing many of them to tears. By now these noises were joined by the sound of cutting tools, hammers and axes that were desperately being used to break up the carriages enough to reach some of the victims.

A shaken young student from Hull Technical College was seen wandering alone around the wreckage looking for his father, who had been with him at the time. Another pupil, this one from

Hymers College, led him away, but it was later found that it was not positive news. Another young boy of 14 years old had his leg jammed under a seat for a long time before they were able to free him. The only time he spoke was to tell them 'don't hurt me' before bravely accepting what was about to happen to him. They eventually managed to free him and the police officer who was with him throughout his ordeal described him to reporters as 'the pluckiest lad I have known'.

Further within the wreckage, a woman known as Mrs Boyd was already dead, her body mutilated and trapped within the twisted remains. The survivors and rescuers were having to navigate around her body in order to continue working to free the living. Incredibly, there were many people who could still walk and they would eventually slowly make their own way out of the train and on to solid ground. There rescuers guided them away, nursing their head wounds, leg trauma, broken bones and internal pain. By now distraught friends and relatives of those on the train were starting to congregate nearby, hoping for news of their loved ones and praying that they had either been saved or missed the train completely.

Those not taken to hospital were taken into local homes. 'The people were awfully kind,' said one survivor. 'Mrs Howes, of 80 Londesborough Street, took me in, dressed a wound on my leg and gave me brandy.'

As the day wore on and the survivors had all been taken away, the railway workers began to gather up all the various personal belongings. The amount of hats without an owner was a sad sight – two bowler hats, two women's hats and five hats belonging to schoolboys, of which the train from Withernsea carried many with their families.

When the final tally was completed, it was found eight had died in the crash, four more later on in hospital, and another two dozen suffered various degrees of injury.

After the rescue operation was finally ended, the investigation could now begin. How could two trains crash into each other on the same track in broad daylight? Colonel J.W. Pringle from the Ministry of Transport led the inquiry, and in just two months his report found the workers at the signal box to blame for sending the Scarborough train on to the wrong track.

Those working at the nearby signal box at Park Street were experienced enough and should have been aware of the standard procedures on trains passing the junctions.

A series of interlocks should have made it impossible to give out a signal unless the route was proved to be safe. With three men in the box, it was found that one of them had simply pulled the wrong lever and had operated the signals for danger while the Scarborough train was still going past; this disengaged a locking bar that allowed the train track to be changed without locking out. The signalmen's aim was to keep the trains moving as smoothly as possible and they didn't want to allow the Withernsea train to delay the Scarborough train for any reason.

The two trains should simply have passed each other, but what had clearly happened at some stage was that a set of slip points was activated that allowed the Scarborough train to move over on to the wrong line and these were controlled by lever number 95 in the signal box. The systems in place made it impossible for the lever to be moved unless lever 171, which controlled the signal faced by the Scarborough train, was also moved.

In the conclusion of his investigation, Colonel Pringle stated that, while one signalman was dealing with the Scarborough departure, another was controlling the Withernsea arrival. The levers he needed to operate were 96 and 97. Lever 171 should not have been returned to danger until the whole train had passed it, by which time it would have cleared the slip points, but, in his hurry to speed things up, the signalman in question moved the lever after only the engine and the first few carriages had passed it.

The other signalman then moved what he thought were levers 96 and 97, but must have been 95 and 96. The slip points controlled by lever 95 were therefore moved during the few seconds between lever 171 being moved and the train reaching the points. By now there was no going back and the two trains were on a collision course.

Both of these signalmen were found to be to blame for the mistakes, one for moving lever 171 too soon and the other for moving lever 95 in error. This was, therefore, just a simple case of being too hasty and complacent in a job that they must have done countless times a day, and in doing so the correct procedure was not followed by the book. Not without sympathy in his summing up, Colonel Pringle blamed the mistake on the anxiety of the signalmen to keep the trains running.

This would not be the only train crash on this line. In 1947 at Burton Agnes station a truck loaded with German prisoners of war ran into the closed gates at the level crossing as the train passed through, killing twelve. In 1986 a similar thing happened at the Lockington level crossing when a small van turned on to the line, which had no barriers at all. The resulting collision derailed the train and killed nine people, including a child in the van. New barriers were installed later and today both disasters have memorials to remember their victims.

On 10 February 2012 a plaque was unveiled behind Hull Royal Infirmary to commemorate the Hull Paragon crash and remember those who died that day. A previous plaque had been stolen several years before, but now this one stands in its place and today overlooks the scene of what is still East Yorkshire's worst rail crash.

Olwen Young got in touch with me during my research into this tragedy and he told me about his great-uncle, who was killed in this crash aged just 17. Philip Escreet and his family lived in Withernsea and every day they would travel by train to their fruit and potato business in Humber Street, Hull. Henry was the father and he would travel together with his sons (he had seven children in total from two marriages) and they would pass the time playing cards together on the journey. Unfortunately, on this day Philip overslept and had to get the later train into Hull, while his father and brother got the usual one. Philip got the train that crashed and so his life ended at such a young age.

As Olwen was growing up, his mother would take him to the back of Hull Royal Infirmary to see the site of the crash and tell the story of how the survivors were taken through the wall and straight into hospital. The confusing part of his story was the fact that the *Hull Daily Mail* had reported completely the opposite of what he was told growing up, that Philip had run for the early train and his father and brother had got the later one, although this would not seem possible with the Withernsea line blocked by the crash. As Philip had slept in, there would be no reason for him to be late and then suddenly be earlier than those going ahead of him! Either way, Olwen was fascinated by the story and was happy that, despite all the family members who had since passed on, his great-uncle would now be remembered in this book.

Near to Philip Escreet's grave in Withernsea churchyard are more than half a dozen others of those who died in the crash that day, many of them referring to them as being victims of the 'Withernsea Rail Disaster', as eleven of the twelve victims came from this small town and only one was from Hull. As there was such a high death toll in such a small area, Withernsea would never forget their residents, the victims of a split-second mistake that had a knock-on effect that spread so far and wide.

9

1939: Sinking of the *Piłsudski*

When a ship the size of an ocean liner sinks off the coast of any country it usually makes headlines and is remembered. Surprising as it may seem, though, this has happened on many occasions around the UK, but because of the fog of wartime reporting, restrictions and bigger stories, many losses have hardly been mentioned ever again. One of these ships was the Polish liner *Piłsudski*.

Built in Monfalcone, Italy, *Piłsudski* was launched on 19 December 1934 for the Gdynia–America Line, which had just recently undergone a major corporate change including the name. She was christened *Piłsudski* after the national hero Józef Piłsudski, who was the country's Chief of State and First Marshal of Poland during the early 1920s. At 14,294 gross tons, the ship was 531ft long and had a beam of 71ft with a capacity to carry around 770 passengers and 350 crew.

With seven decks, she boasted all the luxuries of the other much larger liners as well as all the safety features, just on a smaller scale. She would be joined a few months later by her identical sister ship the *Batory*, and together they would work the North Atlantic routes from Gdynia to the city of New York. This was on top of cruises to the Norwegian fjords and the Caribbean. Her maiden voyage on 15 September 1935 was under the command of 46-year-old Captain Mamert Stankiewicz, a veteran of the Polish military and merchant navy.

The ship's career was a successful one up to the outbreak of the Second World War in September 1939, when she was taken over by the Polish navy and diverted to the United Kingdom to be used as a troopship. Two months later her hull and two funnels were repainted in a dull grey colour scheme and she was made ready for a new task, which would take her from Newcastle all the way to Australia and beyond.

The 180 crew on board were told nothing other than vague mission details: they would arrive in Australia and collect troops. After anchoring in the mouth of the Tyne, the *Piłsudski* finally commenced sailing down the North Sea and by the early hours of 26 November 1939 she was passing Flamborough Head on the East Yorkshire coast. In charge of the ship was Second Officer Jan Michalski, who was checking all around in the dark for other ships passing.

Travelling at just under 20 knots, the ship had two British officers on board as well as her Polish crew and several other UK nationals making up the complement. The *Piłsudski* was running with her lights on to prevent nearby ships colliding with her.

Suddenly, at 05:36 hours, two huge explosions rocked the port side of the ship, one at the bow and the other midships. The stunned officer on the bridge knew that the ship had been hit, whether it be by torpedoes or mines. The ship took on an immediate 10-degree list to port, and the telephone line down to the engine room was put out of action. The captain came up and saw straight away that the ship was doomed, and ordered all personnel to abandon ship via the lifeboats. Judging by the list and the fact that the bow had already started to go down, it looked like the ship was going to sink very quickly and it was only a matter of time before it would be too late to evacuate. The lifeboats were uncovered and within minutes everybody had woken up and had appeared on the upper decks ready to get away to safety. Thankfully there were fewer than 200 people on board; if she had been filled with troops when the explosions happened there could have been thousands of people facing certain death.

Despite the extreme dark and the stormy conditions, all the boats were rigged for lowering, but they were hindered by the crew not being able to see much and when they were sent away they had to contend with the choppy seas. The spray would hit their faces, freezing hands trying to row away from the sinking liner, and the tossing and turning of the boats made it impossible to control them. Remarkably, everyone seemed to be getting off the ship. Second Officer Michalski and the third officer had difficulties with uncoupling some lifeboats but eventually they managed to get away. With the *Piłsudski* now just an empty hulk on the sea, all the survivors could do was wait to be rescued, bobbing about on the rough seas in tiny boats while their huge liner was doomed to sink very soon.

However, as daylight broke that morning, it seemed that the pride of the Polish fleet was not done yet – the *Piłsudski* was still afloat and even looking as if she was moving on to a more even keel. The nearby warship HMS *Valorous* had by now located the boats and started taking on board the survivors, starting with Captain Stankiewicz and two other crew, who were on a raft and in quite a bad state. After being pulled on to the raft by the other crew members, Stankiewicz fought bravely for his life after being wet and cold for several hours, but he sadly died soon afterwards. Press reports later claimed that the final words he spoke were, 'Long live Poland!'

The grey-painted liner was now making her final journey to the seabed as she lurched forward and the gloomy waters covered her hull for the final time. The ship had wallowed in the North Sea for four and a half hours before she went down. It later transpired that she had struck two mines that had been laid by the Germany navy, a terrifying tactic to destroy shipping that would claim so many more vessels on both sides for years to come.

Some 107 survivors were on board the destroyer and these were taken to Hartlepool, while 73 others were taken to Grimsby on board a trawler. The first reports claimed that ten people had been killed in the sinking but it was actually just the captain who had succumbed, and he was later buried with full military honours at West View Cemetery in Hartlepool.

The loss of the *Piłsudski* was a huge blow to the Allied war effort, and within hours the armed merchant cruiser *Rawalpindi* had also been sunk, the week's toll of shipping losses a staggering 100,000 tons. Not a good start to a war that would last six years.

Today the wreck of the *Piłsudski* lies 18 miles from Withernsea at a depth of 108ft and is popular with divers. Her fittings and hull structure are regularly marvelled at, along with her distinctive bow crest. Despite her loss being largely forgotten, she does hold one record – she is still the largest shipwreck off the Yorkshire coast.

10

1952: Farnborough Air Show

In the summer of 2015, the UK was shocked by the news that an aircraft had crashed at the Shoreham Air Show, coming down on a nearby road and killing eleven people who were driving by in their cars. Incredibly, the pilot survived. However, while a headline-hitting disaster like this inevitably stays in the memory of people who were there and saw it, many have forgotten the worst air show crash in Britain in 1952, not long after the Second World War.

The Farnborough Air Show, on the weekend of Friday, 5 to Sunday, 7 September 1952, was going to be an incredible experience. After moving to Farnborough in 1948, the annual SBAC show always saw this north Hampshire town awash with aircraft enthusiasts and visitors, who came for the thrill of watching aircraft put on displays at such close quarters and show off their flying skills. As with previous shows, the new aircraft that heralded the dawn of the jet age stunned the crowds of onlookers with their dramatic displays, which culminated in the breaking of the sound barrier and the coinciding sonic boom. This sound is caused by a jet matching the speed of sound, about 760mph, and the sonic boom is caused by the object creating pressure waves travelling faster than the sound itself can travel.

One of the pilots who was to wow the spectators was 30-year-old test pilot John Derry. For his display on 6 September he was to fly with his flight test observer, Tony Richards, in the new de Havilland DH.110 Jet fighter over the spectators, which would number in excess of 100,000, before climbing to an altitude of around 40,000ft. From here he would dive the aircraft in order to gain speed and travel fast enough to create the sonic boom that everybody so desperately wanted to hear. He had done this a number of times before and had actually become the first person in Britain to break the sound barrier in 1948.

With several huge refreshment tents set up, portable toilets rigged and fencing posted to keep the crowds back, the show got under way. An exhibition hall allowed guests to see for themselves the marvels of engineering and the future of the aviation industry, and also get a chance to talk to the people behind the aircraft. Out in the field where the spectators were watching, thousands of eager onlookers were swaying their bodies and quickly moving their heads backwards and forwards as the might and power of the greatest aircraft in the world shot past with a whoosh. Cheers erupted as the best pilots showed off their seemingly impossible antics and wowed the spectators, making sure that they all felt the price they paid for their tickets was money well spent.

Vic Prior, who was 14 years old, had left his home in Tunbridge Wells on a coach to the Farnborough Air Show. He had been interested in aircraft since he was very young and today he was travelling with friends all around the same age. It was the back end of the school holidays, and what better way to spend one of those last few days than with his friends watching the display. Vic had never been to an air show before and he was very excited as the coach pulled into the grounds. They all got off and made their way as close to the front of the crowd as possible, although with the number of people there that was easier said than done. Vic and his friends tried to get down by the fence but people

Farnborough Air Show, 1952 programme. (Author)

who had been there a lot longer turned them back and sent them up the hill.

Another 14-year-old there that day was Ray Whincup. He too had always had a fascination with anything to do with aviation, and as a reward for his excellent school work that year (ending top of his class at Hunslet Carr School in Leeds), his parents rewarded him by paying for him to travel alone to his uncle and aunt's house in Greenford, Middlesex. From there he travelled to London on the Tube, then caught another train to complete journey to the air show. He recalled:

> It was a very hot day and I was so excited looking around the static displays. Memories of World War Two with the exploits of the Spitfire pilots were still very much in my mind, but now it was the age of the jet and for the first time ever in public, John Derry, Chief Test Pilot of the De Havilland Aircraft Co., was going to attempt to break through the sound barrier in his DH-110.

Ray watched from the side as the other aircraft shot overhead and made the most incredible sounds. The DH.110 was next and everyone was thrilled to see it soar into the sky and make its rapid ascent. But instead of it plunging downwards into a steep dive and making the sonic boom, what happened instead shocked everybody. Ray recalled:

> I was jumping with delight as the double sonic boom echoed over Farnborough as the aircraft broke the sound barrier, and Derry then did a fast, low-level pass in front of delighted spectators, before doing a steep banked turn behind the hangars. Then, to the horror of everyone present, it appeared the engines were too powerful for the airframe, and they broke

away and headed for the crowd. Total panic ensued as it was obvious the 500mph engines were going to hit the crowd. One landed in a car park, killing two persons, and the other hit the crowd, leaving a blackened area of dead and wounded. John Derry and Tony Richards also died in the accident. Within a short space of time the emergency services swung into action, but the need to attend the injured seemed hampered by the scale of the disaster. Anything on wheels was taken over, and the huge containers of ice cream were kicked from sales vans as these vehicles became emergency ambulances. After the initial panic as to where the engines would land it became quite calm, as people looked at each other in shocked disbelief at what had just happened.

Vic Prior noticed that the nosecone came down at the fence near to where they had tried to get in order to see better, while the engines flew over his head and one landed in the car park at the back of them. Incredibly, nobody was injured or killed by those pieces, but if he had not been shooed away by the other onlookers originally, he could have been one of those not going home that day. People in the vicinity rushed over to apply first aid as the mass of injuries overwhelmed the medics that were already there. Scattered wreckage and limbs littered the ground as time became of the essence in getting those people to hospital.

At the other side of the crowd, the shock and suddenness of the disaster was seen in the faces of those who were now stood around too far back to help. The entire episode was caught on camera, looking up at the aircraft high in the sky making its final pass. Viewing it, instead of one object flying across the sky, there are several huge pieces of wing and engine suddenly scattering. They begin to fall, spreading out as two main chunks of wreckage slam harmlessly into the grass, while the third rips into the crowd and kills anything in its path.

After the crash Vic Prior hurried back to the coach, but what confused and surprised him was that the show continued. Neville Duke, another test pilot, took off in his Hawker Hunter and broke the sound barrier himself. While the show went on, the injured were being rushed away to hospital by a fleet of ambulances that were now on the scene. The huge disaster, along with the air show still going on, both confused and wowed the crowd as they didn't know which way to look and what they should be watching.

Ray Whincup remembers this too:

You have to remember that the display was only seven years after World War 2 and the mainly London crowd had been used to bombing raids etc. I remember the announcer saying, 'In the best traditions of British aviation the show will resume as normal in one hour.' One of the items in the display was a new four-engined turboprop airliner. They said it was so safe it could fly on just one engine. To demonstrate they flew about 1,000ft above the crowd and the pilot feathered three engines, causing the airliner to dangle below the remaining engine until he restarted the other engines!

By now it was clear that many people had died. The final count was twenty-nine spectators and the two pilots dead, while more than sixty others were injured. With the day's air display at an end, the victims' relatives now had to pick up the pieces of their shattered lives. Survivors and relatives of the dead were sent messages of sympathy by de Havilland, the Minister of Supply, the Society of British Aircraft Constructors and Her Majesty the Queen.

Vic's coach set off and headed towards the town, where the first chance he got he tried to ring home to tell his parents that he and his friends were safe. Unsurprisingly, he could not get through as all the telephone lines were now busy with thousands of people trying to ring home at the same time. In the meantime, his parents were worried sick; none of the parents would know if their children were safe until they turned up on the doorstep later that day.

Ray had also noticed that long queues had formed at public telephone points, and he could not understand why; the scale of the disaster would not have been fully realised by the people there at this point. When it was announced that the air show would continue he stayed until the end. 'Getting a train back to London took ages and it was after midnight when my ashen-faced aunt and uncle answered my knock at the door. "What's up," I said, and then I realised in the next instant why people had queued up for telephones!'

Vic would later end up in the RAF for his National Service, keeping that love of aircraft alive, although he has been reluctant to visit any air shows since watching the crash that day.

In 1956 Ray was also called up for National Service and served at RAF Patrington. Even these days he has a continued passion for classic aircraft:

In 1997 my wife bought me a trip on Concorde as a 60th birthday present. I have a DVD made from my filming of this event, which includes footage on board as the crew were most helpful. I also filmed the take-off and landing of the same aircraft during the weekend of the event at Leeds. I turn the sound up loud and watch the magnificent aircraft quite often.

An inquest returned verdicts of accidental death on all thirty-one victims of the Farnborough Air Show disaster.

11

1957: Isle of Wight Air Crash

In the early 1950s the area around Calshot in Southampton was home to a very special airport, one that was not home to a normal runway and an aircraft taxiing before a speedy take-off, but one that involved a floating plane speeding along the water before heading skyward. The fleet of flying boats that was berthed there operated a service that sent travellers on journeys all around the world, although there would be a lot of stop-offs at various foreign airports in order to refuel or transfer passengers to connecting flights. This was still a popular service nonetheless.

On Friday, 15 November 1957, the Short Solent Mark 3 flying boat registered G-AKNU was preparing for take-off on a journey to Lisbon, Las Palmas and Madeira with fifty passengers on board and a crew of eight. Her name was the *City of Sydney* and she was one of several owned by Aquila Airways, the company having operated there at Terminal 50 for nine years. Not only that, Aquila was based there with a fleet of flying boats operating services to the Channel Islands and onwards. The terminal had originally been used mostly by BOAC aircraft but they had ceased flying from here by 1950, leaving only two aircraft, *City of*

Sydney and *City of Southampton*, flying from Southampton. Both of these aircraft had since been acquired by Aquila Airways.

That night the plane, piloted by 34-year-old Captain William Eltis, closed the doors with all the passengers ready to fly and started her engines. Moving off from the terminal and given clearance for take-off, the *City of Sydney* picked up speed and sped down Southampton Water, taking to the air at 22:46 for the overnight transit. But something was not right as soon as the aircraft left the water. At 22:54 a radio message from the aircraft simply said, 'Number 4 engine feathered. Coming back in a hurry!' which meant that they had suffered engine failure and were in need of immediate assistance. Turning the flying boat towards Southampton, the *City of Sydney* headed back to the terminal. Those on land were unaware of how bad the problem was but they prepared for an emergency landing all the same. The aircraft banked and was now over the Isle of Wight, only a few miles away from safety.

On the island itself, near the villages of Chessell and Shalcome, three soldiers, Major W.J.F. Weller and Lieutenant J.R. Sherbourn along with company quartermaster Sergeant J.W. Reid, were on a night exercise when they heard the noise of an aircraft in the skies near to their position. What they didn't expect was a sudden huge bang and flash of fire as the aircraft slammed into the nearby chalk cliff in the middle of the fields, the aircraft being almost completely destroyed on impact. Shocked at what they had seen, the three men ran to help but were greeted instantly by a steep slope and the flaming wreckage of the flying boat. The tail had only just survived, that being the most recognisable piece, but incredibly there were survivors in the remains, burned and injured but alive. The men got to work to pull as many people clear of the burning aircraft as possible, but as soon as they got there they knew they were looking at a major disaster. As the flames grew more and more intense, they had to draw back, one of the soldiers having to be held back from going into the wreckage or it would have meant certain death for him.

During their attempts at rescue, the soldiers became exhausted and had burned themselves on the twisted wreckage while trying to access those who were still trapped and people in dire need of medical attention. The blazing fuel everywhere made every movement a risk to their lives as well as the survivors'.

It was not long before word got out that the crash had occurred and rescue services converged on the hillside, but there was very little left to be done except for taking the burned and shattered survivors to be treated. By the morning light, bodies were the only thing left to find and they were recovered as the morning wore on, the nearby army training fort being used as a temporary mortuary where they could be laid out in a row.

When the final death toll was counted up, forty-five of the fifty-eight on board had lost their lives, making this disaster the

Memorial at the site of the Isle of Wight air crash in 2018. (Author)

second-worst air crash in the United Kingdom, and at the time the worst in England. The survivors made it to hospital suffering from horrific injuries, but they would mostly recover. With the horrors of what they saw combined with the broken bones, shattered limbs and horrendous burns, many of them would have to live with the effects for the rest of their lives.

Despite the best efforts of investigators, the cause of the crash was never found; nobody could pinpoint what had caused the engine failure that led to the aircraft diving into a chalk cliff. A public inquiry later drew a blank and officially the reasons behind the case remain unsolved.

The three soldiers who rescued the crash survivors later received awards for their actions that night; Major Weller and Lieutenant Sherbourn received the Order of the British Empire, while company quartermaster Sergeant Reid was awarded the British Empire Medal.

The memories of that disaster were etched into the minds of the residents of the island for years. Marian Coghlan was just 8 years old and living in Newbridge when she heard about it:

As children the local children helped the milkman deliver milk around the village; the morning of the crash the milkman drove over to Shalcombe with a couple of kids on board. You could not see much from the road and, of course, we were not allowed very near. We then had to walk home!

The other thing about the crash is that my Father owned J. Mew & Son haulage and house removal company and one of the furniture vans was used as a temporary morgue on site, until all the bodies could be transferred to St Mary's. Another comment from a local was the smell of burnt bodies, reminiscent of pork. I don't remember [seeing] any smoke, it would have been mid-morning when we were there. I just remembered lots of people milling about. I don't have any recollection of being moved on by police, not like it would have been nowadays!

After a decade of aircraft operations, Aquila Airways soon announced that by July 1958 it would cease operations, nine months after the crash that had cost one of its best aircraft.

A fiftieth anniversary memorial service was held in the village of Brook, Isle of Wight, on 18 November 2007 to commemorate the forty-five who died that day, and in October 2008 a permanent memorial was dedicated at Brook's St Mary's Church, less than a mile south of the crash site. This comprised a small plaque inside the church. There is also a visitors' book and, if you look closely, you will clearly see evidence of those who have come to pay tribute to the victims of the *City of Sydney* crash.

The chalk cliff where the aircraft came down is today accessible from the road and a small monument sits at the base of the hill, commemorating the day when all hell broke loose on a flight to paradise that ended in such peaceful and tranquil surroundings.

12

1968: Ronan Point Collapse

After the Second World War the United Kingdom (as well as many other places) had the huge problem of trying to rehome vast quantities of people in a short space of time. While prefabricated homes were quick and simple to construct, they were not meant to be a permanent fix. The solution was the development of the tower block – a large amount of home space for a great number of people, but at the same time saving valuable land by building upwards instead of across.

The clearing of slum housing and replacing it with a number of twenty-two-storey towers seemed to be the perfect solution, and nine of these buildings were constructed in a small area of Canning Town in East London. Each building could house dozens of families and sort out the major issue that was the overcrowding of the now derelict homes that were scheduled for demolition. The idea was that, over time, the area would be completely revamped and everybody would live in a safe and secure environment.

One of these buildings was Ronan Point on Butchers Road, completed in November 1967 and already occupied by working-class families on the Newham Borough Council housing lists. Named after Deputy Mayor Harry Ronan, this block offered space for several hundred people in its 110 flats, boasting both one- and two-bedroom accommodation. For many this was the perfect home. The towers were cheap enough to make and easy to construct, like a piece of flat-pack furniture made of concrete blocks that slotted into position. However, little did anybody know that this block of flats would soon become famous for the wrong reasons.

It was the early morning of Thursday, 16 May 1968, and people were starting to get up and dressed for work. One of these was 20-year-old machine operator Linda Carter, who worked at Tate & Lyle. Living with her parents, she had a 06:00 shift but always started work at 06:30, and her journey by foot only took around thirty minutes. For months she had watched the high-rise blocks being constructed near their house on Boreham Avenue and was fascinated by just how quickly the work had been progressing.

Her father would always remark to her, 'Look, they've put another floor up already today!' and point out the speed of the building as it soared into the capital's sky.

The early morning quiet was suddenly shattered by an enormous booming. 'I had not heard anything as loud, I thought it was a plane blowing up,' Linda recalls. From her living room she could look out of both the front and back windows. She raced to the front and looked up into the sky but saw nothing.

Running over to the back window, she looked in horror at Ronan Point and watched as the entire corner of the tower block collapsed like a house of cards. She screamed for her dad to come, and he ran in from another room and looked out, shocked at what he was witnessing. Within minutes the damage stretched from the top of the building right down to the ground floor. Dust and smoke clouded the view but it was obvious that there had been a massive structural failure.

They both ran outside to see if they could help. Looking up, Linda watched as a door opened in one of the exposed flats, a woman wearing what seemed to be nightclothes almost stepping out into the void where a room used to be. Pointing up, Linda shouted at her dad, 'There's a woman on the ledge!' but when she looked back the woman must have realised what had happened and backed off and closed the door safely. The experience of watching this woman gave Linda goosebumps.

Linda and her father were among the first people on the scene. The emergency services had not turned up yet and it was so surreal and silent. People were looking out of their flat windows without realising that a chunk of their tower had fallen away completely. For all they knew, the rest of the building was about to collapse with them inside. Families were looking out and all that could be done was to wave at them and tell them to get out of the building. They were confused and couldn't see the danger themselves. At some point a man ran out of the main entrance completely naked and somebody put a blanket around him; he must have had quite a shock by this point.

Amid the noise and the eventual arrival of the emergency services, there was not much Linda and her father could do to help. 'We felt so powerless,' she says. 'Not many people were coming out of the flats and then some were trickling out of the building.' Eventually the tower was evacuated safely and locals took the residents into their homes for somewhere to go. A huge pile of rubble and personal possessions now occupied a large area around the missing floors. Incredibly, the rest of the tower was not in danger of collapsing, but an investigation was launched into why this had happened. It was reported that around eighty families had to be relocated at immediate notice while the tower was assessed.

It also soon became apparent that four people had been killed, a fifth victim succumbing to their injuries in hospital later. Seventeen others were injured.

The cause of the disaster was soon established as being in flat No. 90 on the eighteenth floor, where resident Ivy Hodge had tried to light a match in order to boil water on her cooker, but

The tower block collapse in Canning Town. (Derek Voller, CC BY-SA 2.0 via Wikimedia Commons)

didn't realise that there was a gas leak from a joint in the wall. The resulting explosion blew out the load-bearing walls and caused the rooms above to collapse on top of one another until it took out every floor below, all the way to the bottom. Incredibly, Mrs Hodge was one of those who had survived!

The day after the disaster the TV news teams were all over the area to cover the story. Linda came home after her regular shift to find the BBC were in her house. Her father had talked to presenter Fyfe Robertson while he was outside and offered to host him and his camera crew for refreshments. They asked if they would be allowed to use his house as a base for their comings and goings while the story was being covered and he gladly agreed. By now half of them were sitting around while her mum was frying up bacon sandwiches for them.

There was talk of renovating the tower block and allowing people back in. Linda's sister-in-law lived in Ronan Point with her two children and she saw with her own eyes a large gap appear in her wall with water coming through, right next to where the flats had collapsed. After seeing this, she vowed that she would never live in a tower block again. The stress from watching this unfold saw her come out in a rash that her doctor said was a nervous reaction. For quite a while after she just simply broke down and cried.

Thinking about Ronan Point today, Linda says that she will never forget the noise she heard as the rooms collapsed. 'I can still hear the noise today; it makes you go cold thinking about it.'

An inquiry was launched into the construction methods used, and this highlighted so many issues it became more of a scandal that this was allowed to happen. Radical changes were needed to ensure that something so disastrous could not happen again. New legislation was brought into force and inspections of high-rise buildings became stricter.

The collapse of Ronan Point was a shocking wake-up call to those trying to cut corners when building high-rise accommodation. The slot-together type of construction that was simply bolted together was flawed and, as this incident has shown, massively unsafe. However, despite the disaster, it would be 1986 before the building, along with the other eight blocks around it, was finally condemned and the locals were finally able to breathe a sigh of relief.

When the building was being demolished, they took it apart piece by piece in order to examine it. The issues with its construction were plain to see and it shocked everybody who saw it. Never again would such sloppy construction be allowed.

Tower blocks continue to be home for thousands of people in the UK today, and while many of them are perfectly safe, in recent years a spate of fires has highlighted them as potential death traps due to the flammable cladding that has been used to upgrade their appearance.

The worst of these incidents occurred on 14 June 2017, when a small fridge fire at Grenfell Tower in the Kensington area of London turned into a raging inferno as flames crept up the outside wall and killed seventy-two people. The cladding is said to have fuelled the fire and once again opened the debate about the safety of tower blocks.

It is only as we see the outcome of this inquiry that we can see if any new lessons can be learned – or if the old ones are being ignored.

13

1970: Explosion in the Hull Underpass

The city of Hull, as covered in the chapter on the rail disaster, has been at the forefront of the fishing industry for centuries. As one of the main trawler bases of the infamous Cod Wars of the 1970s against the Icelandic fishing vessels, which led to frantic battles out at sea in which these huge ships clashed and rammed each other, the city saw a decline in the industry as the main source of income, and over the decades the trawlers slowly left the docks and many of the businesses shut down.

St Andrew's Dock today are abandoned, the buildings a derelict mess of broken windows, graffiti and used needles left by drug addicts. Just behind the Lord Line building – a huge four-storey block that was once a bustling office and headquarters – lies a pedestrian walkway that runs through an underpass. The busy roadway of the A63 Clive Sullivan Way lies overhead, one of the main roads into the city from the south-west. The concrete walls are now only frequented by people wanting a shortcut from the industrial area to the St Andrews Quay Retail Park or by the occasional dog walker, but few realise that a major incident happened there that shocked the city and led to Humberside Police mourning a personal loss.

It was Friday, 23 October 1970, and it was pay day for the fishermen. The docks were a hive of activity all the time and today was no exception. Five decades ago this was a road tunnel and it was quite common for cars and vans to transit through to and from the docks. One of the fishermen that day was 38-year-old Ray Wilkinson, who was walking back from collecting his wages with his 3-year-old daughter Nicola. As usual, she was lagging behind him as he walked ahead. They lived on St Georges Road, which was a walk of just over half an hour back to their house where his wife was waiting for him. Normally he would have got his pay, known as his 'settings', the day before, but it had been busy with his vessel coming in only hours before and he had ended up leaving it until the day after. That morning they had got up late and his other daughter, 8-year-old Jackie, was going to school. Normally they got a taxi to the dockyard and dropped her off at school on the way but today they had to walk.

Dozens of people were walking around this area, and a British Transport Police constable, 22-year-old Keith Winter, was on duty nearby at a checkpoint. He had been married just five months and his wife, too, was waiting at home for him in the nearby town of Beverley. He had joined the police as a cadet at Hull Docks in 1964 and became constable by 1967. It was common for the BTP to have officers at the docks and today was just another day.

At just after 11:00, a truck carrying a huge, white, 500-gallon tank of propane gas was travelling along the road heading towards the docks but the driver did not realise how low the underpass was. As the pressurised cylinder passed under, the valve at the top of the gas tank hit the concrete roof and ruptured the container. It immediately began leaking its deadly cargo. The truck stopped suddenly and became trapped in the tunnel, where a cyclist was passing by smoking a cigarette. By this time, it was too late.

Another truck was coming from the opposite direction and shut off its engine; the escaped gas fed it and kept the engine running.

Hull underpass in 2020, fifty years after a huge explosion killed two and injured seventeen. (Author)

When the second driver realised what was happening, he got out and ran as fast as he could.

An almighty boom echoed as a fireball tore through the tunnel. Ray would always remark that it 'blew us off our feet' as everybody within the area was engulfed in flames. The cyclist seemed to burst into flames as the gas ignited. PC Winter ran down to assist but within seconds he too was on fire.

The shockwave reverberated across the streets either side, blowing out the windows of the nearby shops just 33yd away from the tunnel, the newspaper shop suffering damage as glass flew inside.

Ray had to think fast. He grabbed Nicola and ran as fast as he could to try to beat the flames, but both of them were on fire. Heading to the policeman's box nearby, he knew he couldn't outrun the burning sensation but he had to try. By the time he reached the fresh air he was left with only his underwear elastic around him; his body and that of his daughter were very badly burned. As he ran out of the flames people ran away in terror at the sight of this naked man covered in flames; the sheer horror of what they saw sent everybody into shock. Ray quickly threw Nicola like a rugby ball over to a Mr Kirk so that she could be taken away safely. He was now in a bad state, with burns all over his hands and face.

Incredibly, a rush decision earlier that day had saved his daughter. As they had been getting ready that morning he had thrown Nicola her older sister's Ladybird coat, and she had put it on without question. With a five-year age gap, the coat was way too big, but the miracle was that this coat just happened to be flame retardant – an unusual feature in 1970 for a child's coat. Because of the size of it, the flames caught only her exposed skin and the rest of her body was saved. It was later found that, if she had suffered the same level of burns as her father, she would not have survived the disaster. She was cared for in the nearby policeman's hut until help arrived.

Twenty-three-year-old Keith Ward was also in the tunnel that day and it was only by chance that he was walking alone. His nephew had woken up with the measles, so his fiancée Dorothy stayed at home to look after him. He was caught up in the blast and was now in a bad state.

Incredibly, the gas truck driver was uninjured, but nineteen people were now needing urgent medical attention. The nearby Fish Dock Medical Centre took in the injured until the ambulances arrived, then they were whisked off as fast as possible to Hull Royal Infirmary, where they could be treated for the horrendous burns they had suffered.

Fire teams were on scene and the fire had been extinguished but the tanker still needed to be made safe, so water was sprayed on the cylinder to cool it down. The last thing anyone wanted was the entire tanker going off as that would wipe out half of the docks.

Anything that made a spark or a naked flame was banned from the area and cars were held back for a half-mile radius.

Police officer Norman Woollons was sent over to the tunnel to give a hand with several other officers, and one image stuck in his head that day. 'I do remember seeing the policeman's helmet lying in the tunnel … Very sad, and my first taste of operational police work.'

Ray's wife Mavis was working in the docks at the time, on the factory floor. She had worked in the fishing industry her entire life, and so when two police officers walked across to see her she knew something was not right. They broke the news to her that Ray and Nicola had been in an accident and she was immediately taken to Hull Royal Infirmary. She was led into the resuscitation room on the Accident and Emergency ward and she was so taken aback by the state of her daughter's body that she swore that it was not her. The right side of her face had taken the full brunt of the blast and her eyes were damaged. Thankfully, because of the coat, everything from her wrists down to her knees was unaffected. As Mavis walked around the wards she saw the police officer laid out, several others nearby and the putrid smell of burning flesh permeated her nostrils. 'I will never forget that until the day I die,' she said years later. What was even worse was the state of Ray's head: it was swollen to the size of a football.

She had to make a difficult decision, for the doctors had to transfer Nicola to Pinderfields Hospital in Wakefield, where there was a specialist burns unit. It would have been a case of her needing to split her time between Pinderfields for Nicola and Hull Royal for Ray. Faced with such a dilemma, she spoke to the doctors and consultants and they managed to get permission to carry out Nicola's skin grafts in Hull so that both could be kept at the same hospital. It was here that their doctor, Mr Campbell, conducted some of his first work and later would become one of the leading plastic surgeons for burns units in the country.

Keith Ward's fiancée Dorothy had gone home after looking after her nephew and heard the phone ring. She picked it up to find that it was Keith's father, Edward, to say that he had been in an accident. All the police could say was that he was in Hull Royal Infirmary but it seemed as if it wasn't serious. She went around to his parents' house to await news as the hospital was so crowded with people that there was no way they could get in.

Eventually the hospital allowed immediate relatives to see the casualties, but unfortunately this did not include Dorothy as she was not married to him. When his father looked at how bad his injuries were, he collapsed with shock. The hospital staff asked Dorothy who she was and eventually allowed her to go in to see him. She too was shocked at what she saw. All around her were victims of the blast, four of them with two nurses per bed at all times. She saw that each person had a head that seemed bigger than normal, swelled to three times the size.

The doctors told them to prepare for the worst as Keith was not expected to survive. Not only had he suffered 80 per cent burns but he had also ingested fumes that had burned his insides. The state of his hands, face, head, legs and back was devastating. Thankfully he was unconscious and his family were now coming to terms with the fact that he may never wake up.

But, incredibly, Keith did survive. For the next six weeks he would remain in Hull Royal Infirmary, his condition too fragile to be transferred to the burns unit at Pinderfields Hospital, which is where the others were being taken. He was fed pureed meals through a straw and was eventually deemed fit enough to be sent to Pinderfields, where he remained for the next four months. His eyes had to be sewn shut as he had lost his eyelids, skin grafts eventually giving him his sight back even after an infection had meant doctors had to carry out the procedure twice.

Twenty-four hours after the blast, 49-year-old Norman Brooks became the first fatality of the Hull explosion when he died in hospital of his injuries. Despite all efforts to save him, PC Keith Winter also died of his injuries on 23 November, exactly a month after the explosion.

Four days later, a funeral service took place for him at Beverley Minster, attended by police officers from across the county as well as many of the dock managers and staff at Hull Royal Infirmary. His coffin was taken to Queensgate Cemetery nearby and interred.

But that wasn't the end of his story. His family wanted something to remember him by and so donated a trophy in his name to the police. From 1971 until 1984 the Keith Winter Cup was awarded to the probationer who achieved the highest marks during their training. This was suspended when the training system was changed, but was reinstated in 1992, with the approval of the original donors. The cup was rededicated as an award for excellent police work by a probationary constable and is still awarded today.

Ray Wilkinson's family were shocked at hearing the news that he and Nicola had been caught up in the blast. The day after, the whole family were due to attend the wedding of Nicola's aunt and uncle, and Nicola's mother insisted that they should carry on with it in their absence. It was a shame because, despite her injuries, Nicola could not stop talking about it and so they arranged a party for her when she eventually got out of hospital, which was highlighted in the newspapers the day after.

Nicola saw a psychiatrist to help her cope with her injuries but this didn't seem to make much difference. Her father, who struggled to live with what had happened, constantly blamed himself for his daughter being placed in danger. Not that he could have predicted what happened, but survivor's guilt is common when others have been injured or killed, especially when the injured party is someone's own flesh and blood.

Ray's injuries affected him throughout his life. His hands were badly burned and he did not regain full use of them for several years. After spending a long time in and out of the hospital, Ray was finally discharged, but never went back to sea on the trawlers again. Instead he received some compensation and used it to open two shops near the docks, before he ended up being a security guard.

I asked Nicola how it had affected him over the years: 'Dad talked about it, it was never a secret. We always talked about it together. I had skin grafts on my face and head, and the thickness of the skin on that part of my body was now very thin so Dad was very protective. He wouldn't let me do certain things in case I fell and cut my head.'

The psychological trauma of such an event would be high-lighted today, but back in 1970 this was barely an afterthought for many. Nicola Wilkinson has no memory of the explosion or her time in hospital, but she has a deep-rooted dislike for tunnels and does not like going on the London Underground on her own as the lights disturb her but she can't explain why. Another subconscious reaction is that the sound of chips being put in a chip pan gives her a sickening feeling in her stomach. For years her mother had to give her a warning that she was putting some chips on so that she did not start getting anxious. She was 36 years old when her father told her that it was the exact same noise that the tanker made as the gas was escaping right before the explosion. The sight and sound of a coal fire so affected her that she did not have one in her house until she was 47. She also has to take charge of any gas-powered barbecue, otherwise she feels very anxious.

For many years a carrier bag containing the coat that she wore that day and the charred leather shoes that she had on her feet were kept as evidence to be used in any compensation claim or court case that may or may not emerge in the future.

Nicola spent her childhood within walking distance of the site of the blast in the Hessle Road area and had a lot of nightmares when she was small. Her friends wanted to skateboard down the tunnel but she would avoid it, and as the years went by the tunnel was eventually gated off for a long period of time. The scars on Nicola's face led to her being bullied at school because of the way she looked, but she came out fighting and learned to stand up for herself. It got worse when she moved to another estate and the teacher stood her up in front of the class on the first day to talk about her injuries. 'Mum had to tell them about the scars and the school must have thought it was a good idea, but I just felt embarrassed.' The scars on her hands are still visible today, and as she worked over the years she had to hide them in photographs. She received compensation when she turned 18, but this was only around £2,000 – nothing compared to what you would get today if you take into account the psychological scars.

Mr Kirk, the man who took her in his arms that day in the policeman's box, met her again when she was 16 years old. He ran a club at the nearby Boulevard, just up the road from the tunnel, and she went in with her parents to meet him for the first time in thirteen years. Although her memory of this day had faded completely, she still found this meeting very emotional as she was able to hear the story of what he did for her and she could thank him personally.

It was what her mother went through that stuck with her, though: 'I can't imagine being in that situation with my children, I can't imagine what that must feel like, to see your own child that you don't recognise.'

Her mother carried on working within the fishing industry and the factory floors were her way of life for years. She passed away aged 67 in 2007. Her father Ray was very close to her over the years. He had not been to work for two years after the disaster, and when he finally managed to get on a bike and cycle to the docks again, he was found sitting on the other side of town on a grass verge, wondering what he was doing there. The trauma of that day stayed with him until he eventually died in 2010 at the age of 73, still feeling the guilt for the injuries his daughter had received.

Keith Ward eventually left hospital but he would continue to attend appointments for many years for skin treatment and hair transplants. This affected his confidence and he said that he didn't like to go out with his head looking like it did, as he didn't like people staring at his injuries. His mental health suffered and he spiralled into depression, not being able to work for ten years due to his physical and psychological injuries. A loud bang would make him jump and he could not cook a joint of pork as it would remind him of what it smelled like when he was on fire. It would be more than thirty years before he could tolerate fireworks going off, and he would tell his grandchildren about what happened when they asked about his injuries. At one point he even did a couple of talks to other burns victims at Pinderfields Hospital at their request.

What was incredible is that, due to the extent of his burns, the operations performed on him were filmed for training purposes to show students and other doctors how they were done. The knowledge obtained from this came in extremely useful in July 1988 when the *Piper Alpha* oil rig exploded in the North Sea, and once again mass burns casualties flooded the hospitals.

The doctors told Keith that his survival was a miracle, but his treatment meant that his lifespan would not be a long one. Once again he defied the odds and lived until he was 70 years old, passing away in 2017.

The people of Hull walk past this area now without a thought as to what happened fifty years ago, and for the few people who do remember it is now a distant memory. Steven Lindstrom contacted me during the research for this book and told me that his late father, George Alan Lindstrom, was a colleague of PC Winter and he remembers the shock his family endured when they found out. This was not least because George had relieved Keith on the earlier shift and it could so easily have been him. George was one of those attending the funeral a month later. 'I don't recall him later ever talking much about it. He stoically resumed his duties, being of a generation who had come through similar incidents years earlier,' Steven said, referring to the Second World War bombing raids.

Today the tunnel has been modified, as has the road, and traffic can no longer pass through. The underpass is now deserted, the docks abandoned, and the whole area is due for redevelopment. No plaque stands here today to tell the story of what happened; only those who were there will know the true horror of the biggest explosion Hull had seen since the Second World War.

14

1971: Clarkston Gas Explosion

The Scottish city of Glasgow is steeped in history and surrounding the city, at short distances, are towns that have their own communities; Clarkston is one of them. A suburban town in East Renfrewshire, with amenities that support the surrounding villages, the population here is a close-knit 20,000.

On Thursday, 21 October 1971, the afternoon traffic was at a normal pace for a regular working day, and a strip of shops along Busby Road were open for business. This area consisted of a number of businesses in a row with an overhead car park making up the roof of the shops, the road leading up to it a curved ramp on a steep incline. The previous day these shops at Clarkston Toll had reported a strong smell of gas and as a result engineers from Scottish Gas had been sent to investigate. They searched in vain for the location of the smell, returning again on the Thursday to carry on with their search.

Little did they realise that there was a gas leak beneath these shops, originating at the gas main that was underneath the very places where shoppers were now going about their business. Nearby, a bus was passing in front of the shops.

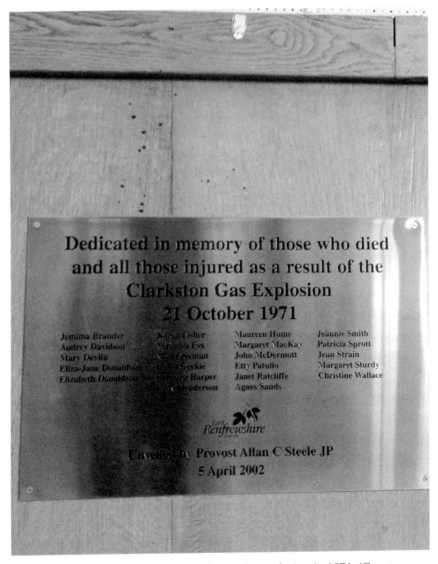

Dedicated in memory of those who died
and all those injured as a result of the
Clarkston Gas Explosion
21 October 1971

Jemima Brander	Karen Fisher	Maureen Hume	Jeannie Smith
Audrey Davidson	Veronica Fox	Margaret MacKay	Patricia Sprott
Mary Devlin	Ann Freeman	John McDermott	Jean Strain
Eliza-Jane Donaldson	Helen Geekie	Etty Patullo	Margaret Sturdy
Elizabeth Donaldson	Flora Harper	Janet Ratcliffe	Christine Wallace
	Henderson	Agnes Sands	

*East
Renfrewshire*

Unveiled by Provost Allan C Steele JP
5 April 2002

Clarkston Hall plaque to those lost in the nearby explosion in 1971. (Courtesy Chris MacInnes)

At around 14:50 the slow leak of gas had built up, and all it took was a small naked flame from somewhere in the area for a huge explosion to rip the entire street apart. Fifteen shops were devastated, the car park collapsed on top of people, the passing bus was hit by flying wreckage and masonry, and the blast sent a wave of devastation completely wrecking 100yd of street.

As large pieces of wreckage landed, dust and smoke billowed into the air, and those caught up in the blast wondered what had just happened as they staggered around injured, bleeding from wounds, with broken bones and many suffering from concussion.

Twenty-nine-year-old Catherine (not her real name) was working at an ironmongers on the long strip of shops at the time. Suddenly the blast blew the door open but, because its centre was far enough away, she was not injured by anything flying into the shop. She walked out of the front door and was greeted by complete silence, with not even the birds making a noise. At a nearby hairdressers people came running out with their hair still in rollers to see what had happened. A dress shop had broken windows and a woman was being helped outside.

Catherine described what had happened below ground:

At pavement level there was a berm, or slope, down towards the railway at the rear. At one spot, there was a wall built into the berm so that a full basement could be built for the dress shop. The rest had half basements, good only for cellar use. The explosion hit that wall and bounced back, so that the supports for the cellar areas were destroyed. That caused the ground floor area to collapse, which in turn caused the ground floor to fall into the basement/void area, followed by the car park above. That wall saved the three or four shops at the top.

A bus had stopped at the bottom end to let a passenger off. That passenger was killed instantly. I remember a girl helping a lady out of the dress shop through the broken window. I had been in that dress shop basement, which was the children's department, in the morning talking to Helen, the supervisor. I was picking up clothes for my kids that I had put on hold. Helen was a very nice and accommodating lady. She subsequently died of her injuries. I think there was another person with her at the time who was killed instantly. All night, we could hear the sound of the machines looking for bodies. I never worked in any of those shops again.

Eleven-year-old Karen Lund was at Netherlee Primary School when she saw blue flashing lights and heard the sirens of almost two dozen ambulances heading towards Clarkston. This was something that the young girl would always remember.

Elaine Graham was a 16-year-old receptionist at Lower Clyde Water Board and this was her first day on the job. She would often see the workers going in and out of her offices, a collection of blue huts situated on Burnfield Road just before the railway bridge. Their job was to deal with any water issues on the south side of Glasgow, and they were often called on to deal with what seemed to be never-ending issues such as discoloured water and problems with the supply.

Suddenly news about the explosion in Clarkston came on the radio and everyone who heard it stopped their own jobs and rushed down to the scene to help in any way they could. When they reached the scene it was utter chaos. By now the initial shock of the blast had gone and it had been replaced by the screams of those trapped under a mountain of rubble. The rescuers dug away with their bare hands, hoping to reach those that were still alive under the concrete. The car park had taken the full brunt of the explosion and was now flattened on top of drivers and their cars. There were so many the rescuers could not reach and their cries for help would haunt them.

That afternoon the water board staff would return to their offices looking exhausted. Their efforts to rescue survivors were overtaken in their minds by the image of bodies being loaded on to ambulances. They looked shattered and were visibly shaken by what they had seen. The Salvation Army had turned up to feed and water the teams and to contact loved ones to tell them that they were OK. The whole area was stunned by what had happened, the emergency services now managing to reach the survivors but alas with more bodies located along the way.

When everything was finally cleared of people, the entire street was a shocking mess. Collapsed buildings and wrecked cars littered the entire area, wreckage and rubble from the blast had ended up in every direction and businesses were ruined. Some would not open again after this disaster; others would be closed for months until rebuilding work could be carried out. Over the coming days, several people who were taken to hospital died of their injuries, until eventually there was a final death toll of twenty-two people.

But it could have been even worse, as Catherine says:

Had the explosion happened a couple of hours later, the result would probably have been much worse. It was common during the week for the pavement outside that row of shops to be filled with schoolchildren, almost all teenagers, coming home from the nearby secondary school. There was a café as well as a bakery on that strip. On top of which, it was the natural route home for a large number of them. If I recall correctly, it happened on a Thursday, which was NOT a normal shopping day for most. Had it been Friday at say 4 p.m., it would have been much worse. In addition, it was, or had been, raining that day, which also discouraged many from going out.

An inquiry with a jury was set up and in January 1972 it heard evidence from metal experts who stated that the gas pipes had a combination of stress and corrosion, which had led to the eventual leaking out of gas and filling of the void spaces over time. Add that to the fact that the initial laying of the pipes may have contributed to them becoming weaker and factor in the vibrations caused by the traffic in the streets above, then you have a ticking time bomb waiting to go off. It was just bad luck that the leak was not found in time; instead the gas in the air was eventually turned into an inferno by a spark from an unknown source.

On 10 February the jury decided that no particular person was to blame for the disaster, highlighting a few recommendations for the gas companies and stating that the source of the ignition was, and still is, not known to this day.

Eventually the street was rebuilt with shops in the exact same style as before and the car park above was once again opened for business. Today you can walk around that area fifty years after the event without even a hint that a major disaster had taken place here, until you reach the last shop before the car-park ramp. On the wall next to this end shop is a small silver plaque that simply says, 'This marks the site of the Clarkston Gas Explosion 21st October 1971', and directs visitors to a further memorial in the nearby Clarkston Hall. This second plaque lists all twenty-two victims and both were unveiled on the same day in April 2002. Everybody in that area remembers what happened that day but nobody can relive the devastation like the heroes who dropped their tools and ran to help, saving countless lives and showing that, when the chips are down, humanity is at its best.

15

1975: Dibbles Bridge Coach Crash (2)

Fifty years had passed since the first Dibbles Bridge coach crash, the event and the victims all but forgotten about, with only a few people remembering what happened on that lonely road. The world had changed a lot since then. There had been another world war and many more coach crashes, with much higher death tolls, that had long since overshadowed the charabanc disaster.

One of those who didn't forget was Basil Cardus. His father, Harry, had seen the devastation of the 1925 crash and had told Basil about it over the years. Now his father had passed away at the age of 72 in 1964, and since then Basil had always thought of the story, especially when incidents happened at that bridge. In the early 1970s he saw the wreckage of 16 tons of steel plates that went over the edge; in another near disaster he saw coal, which had come off the back of a lorry as it took the bend, almost send the entire truck over; and another coach had smashed into the wall but thankfully carried on its journey with nobody injured.

On 27 May 1975, Basil was living up in the nearby village of Hebden, at Turfgate Farm, which he had purchased five years before. Although he was not a farmer himself, he contracted out his land to those who did farm and got working himself on the

Dibbles Bridge coach crash, 1975. Almost fifty years to the day after seven people had died in a similar accident, thirty-three were killed in a pensioners' outing. Compare the photo of the 1925 crash to see just how similar the crashes were. (Courtesy Mirrorpix/Reach Licensing)

land clearing the stones and draining water from the fields. Today was a beautiful summer's day and he was working at home in his garage, the view of the entire area as amazing as ever – and as quiet as it ever had been. He had a view of the nearby main road, now called the B6265, and his mind was on the job in hand when he went over to the other side of the garage to get a tool. As he looked up he saw something odd: a huge cloud of dust over the fields towards the road. He knew then that this time it wasn't a near collision; this looked like something more serious.

He got into his car to head over to investigate. This was still a very quiet lane with little traffic. Not much had changed in the last fifty years, so if something was amiss then they would need all the help they could get. As he drove down he saw a local lad named Richard Wallace, who was coming up the hill to call for ambulances.

'What's gone off?' Basil shouted to him.

'A coach has gone through!' he replied.

Basil continued driving down towards the bridge, not truly believing that something like this could actually happen again.

Parking his car at the farm by the side of the road about 175yd away from the bridge, he walked down and saw that the entire parapet had gone, just like his father had described five decades earlier. The dust had settled by now but as he looked over the edge he was met by a scene of utter devastation. A few people were already down there: some lads from Hull who had been camping nearby had raced over to help. Police officer John Middleton had hurried over as soon as he had been called. He had only been there by chance as he was filling in for an officer who was not able to come to work that day.

In the area below, a modern coach was upside down, its wheels in the air, its body broken and flattened on the dry-stone wall. It was an almost exact replica of the scene that Basil's father had faced.

That morning had started out as an exciting day for the pensioners in the town of Thornaby at the very top of the county of North Yorkshire. The 09:00 departure from the town centre was the culmination of a planned outing to the Yorkshire Dales by 62-year-old former Mayoress Dorothy White, who had spent the last thirty years organising coach trips for the locals to get them out and socialising together. She was a popular woman who never failed to deliver a great time and the trips were often very sought after when they were announced.

Today the forty-five-seat Bedford Duple coach, owned by local company Riley's Luxury Coaches, would be driven by security guard and part-time driver Roger Marriott, who was making the journey with his wife Joan close by. The 8-year-old coach had a safety feature that meant, if it should suffer brake failure on the front brakes, the back-wheel brakes that the coach was also fitted with would enable the vehicle to slow down and stop safely.

But as Roger lay in the wreckage dying, his last words to a rescuer were simply, 'My gears were a bit sticky and my brakes just failed.' He died on the scene moments later.

By now Basil had made his way down the hill to the wreckage of the coach, and straight away he saw two or three people lying dead or unconscious face down, with the rest still trapped inside the bus. He walked around the wreckage to see if there was an easy way to get any of them out, the chilling part being that there were no screams, crying or even whimpering. 'It was like walking around a graveyard, total silence from them. You'd have thought there would be some noise but there was nothing, I couldn't believe it.'

He knew that there was nothing he could do with that amount of weight covering the victims, so he headed back home to get a tractor and jack in case that would be able to assist. He had a four-wheel drive with a loader and digger attached, but this wouldn't do any good, he thought. Instead, he rang up the nearby garage and told them to bring a tow truck with a winch on that could lift 20 tons. But by this time there were so many emergency teams on the scene that they couldn't even get close. There were so many people you could barely move.

At this point people were entering the coach through the broken windows. Inside was a mass of bodies and there was nothing they could do but try to get them out if they showed any signs of life. The ambulance teams managed to get all those still living out of the bus and headed to Airedale Hospital, Basil helping carry the stretchers up the road. Some of the ambulances backed right down to a cottage near the crash site so that the injured could be put straight in the back. Too many people were now on the scene, and Basil realised he had done all he could so reluctantly headed back home.

One of the police officers on site that day was Kevin Hullah, a constable with Northallerton traffic division who had joined the force in March 1970, and he loved his job. At 23 years old he was married with a 1-year-old daughter, living in a police house, and today he was on the A1 near Dishforth escorting an abnormal load, a transformer on a low-loader. On the police radio he had heard a lot of talk about a major accident at Dibbles Bridge involving a bus and that Sergeant Jack Matthewman, the Skipton traffic officer, had answered the call and headed to the scene. As soon as Sergeant Matthewman arrived he realised that this was a huge job and called immediately for supervision, senior officers, ambulances, fire brigade and recovery vehicles. Kevin was shocked to hear that a coach full of people had overturned, and as soon as Inspector Harry Furnace heard the same message he responded by telling all units to head to the scene if they were able to do so. Kevin got on the radio straight away: 'I have an abnormal load but can drop him off at the café, The Windmill Café, at Rainton on the southbound carriageway of the A1 at Dishforth.'

They gave him the go ahead and he pulled the lorry over and explained, 'I have got an RTA to go to, I'm going to have to leave you here.'

Leaving the lorry, Kevin hit the road again with sirens blaring and blue lights flashing and raced through Ripon. He was alone in his car, which was quite common back in the 1970s, and he arrived at the scene in just fifteen minutes. He was unfamiliar with the area but soon realised that he had reached the right site when he counted no fewer than twenty-two ambulances, plus police and fire vehicles, crammed together for hundreds of yards around the accident.

Parking as close as he could to the bridge, he walked the rest of the way and was shocked by the sight of the coach lying upside down, the bridge brickwork destroyed. One of those directing the operation was Inspector Pete Wilkinson, who had a reputation for being a laid-back man, and it was this attitude that led to quick and sensible decisions being made throughout his career; for this his subordinates thought he was 'a diamond guy'.

As the afternoon wore on, the crane company Elmsleys had started lifting the wreckage slowly to allow the teams further access to the coach inside so they could continue the recovery of bodies. What struck those on the scene was the personal items that were now littering the cottage garden – clothing, handbags, shoes, items from what should have been a happy day out. All of this had to be gathered together, which Kevin did without question. Others were scrambling around in the wreckage hoping to find more people to pull out alive. But all they were finding now were bodies, which were put on stretchers and taken to the side of the river bank and laid out covered in blankets.

When all the survivors had been accounted for, police officers were allocated to an ambulance each to escort two bodies to Airedale Hospital mortuary in Keighley. Kevin found that he had three in his ambulance, two on the benches and one laid out on the floor. One of these bodies was the driver, Roger Marriott. As the convoy of ambulances went through the tiny villages, the people outside a pub looked on in shock as they all drove past together, wondering what had happened that so many were needed. They would soon find out as the news was breaking on the television bulletins and the radio would by now be giving updates in the hourly broadcasts.

As the ambulances pulled into the hospital, the bodies were taken inside and the post-mortems were conducted straight away due to the severity of the disaster and the fact that so far more than twenty bodies had been counted, with more due in. The first thing to be established was that there was nothing physically wrong with the driver and that his final words actually described the cause of the crash. Kevin went through his clothing for personal effects and found a police warrant card – he was a special constable in Cleveland and he carried his ID at all times. He took all the things he could find, as well as his clothing, and bagged them up. Test results came back to show that the driver was in good health and there was no alcohol in his system. That crossed out the easy theory that the driver was the cause, which has to be considered in any road traffic accident; now they could concentrate on the vehicle itself.

What they did find was that the bodies were all virtually intact; it was mostly crush injuries and fractures but they were in one piece. Kevin had to stay with his three bodies until the very end and the medical staff were finished examining them. When he was finally allowed to go, transport then had to be arranged for all the officers who were now stranded at the hospital, as their patrol cars were still parked up at Dibbles Bridge where they had left them.

It was around 23:00 that night that he finally got back to his car. When he returned to the station he was met by Harry Furnace and David Burke, both high-ranking officers who had got a crate of beer for the officers, handing the drinks out for a job well done and to thank them for everything they had done that day in the exceptional circumstances. Kevin was on a 10:00 to 18:00 shift that day so he was well into his off watch, bearing in mind that he had to start early the day after as he was on the 06:00 shift.

Meanwhile, in the town of Thornaby, the residents were hearing the dreadful news that the bus had crashed and people had been killed. Eileen Dobson had known about these trips and had even been on them herself sometimes. At 34 years old, she was now at home with her 10-year-old son Stephen, but her mother-in-law was on the coach. Edna Dobson had been a widow since her husband had passed away in 1967. She used to love going on these trips and was a regular participant in the pensioner parties and visits. She had three sons, all grown up and with lives of their own, her eldest being Eileen's husband.

But as Eileen settled down to watch the BBC news, the information filled her with horror. She knew instantly that the crash involved the coach that the women from her town were on. Not just Edna but pretty much all the people on the coach were known to her, three of them from the same street as herself.

Immediately she ran over the road to ask a neighbour to watch her son and then went to see her brother-in-law, to use his phone to get more information. Her husband, Thomas, was in the nearby shipyard working oil rigs and was uncontactable at this time, so a neighbour went around to go and get him for her. At this point they had no idea who was alive and who was dead. They found out that the survivors were being taken to Airedale Hospital, so she and the rest of the family, including Thomas, who had now raced home from work, headed to Keighley, not knowing what awaited them when they got there.

It was a journey that had all their minds racing, wondering what was going on. So little information was being released as the authorities simply did not know enough. When they got to the hospital there was a crowd of people desperate for news. The crowd parted to one side to let them through and they were taken into the wards where the survivors were being treated.

Edna lay in bed, one of several in a row of patients who were all badly bruised from head to foot, but incredibly there was not a broken bone among them. She was still very shook up and had no idea what had happened. She must have lost consciousness in the crash and woke up in what looked to her like a field, having been already pulled out of the wreckage by the rescue teams.

This would be the first of ten days in hospital for Edna. She kept asking about the other ladies on the coach, but there only seemed to be around a dozen in the hospital out of a bus full of people. Eileen found out about them on Edna's behalf and a nurse told her who had died. The scale of the disaster was shocking, but she needed to keep a straight head and asked where Edna's shopping bag was being kept. Inside it were her house keys and she needed to get her a change of clothes. She was directed to a nearby church hall, where personal items were all laid out for people to come and identify. She eventually found the bag and the keys were safely inside. Dorothy White's bag contained a lot of money. As the organiser, she would collect payment from those travelling on the day of the trip and tick off the names in her little book. Eileen can still see all those items in the church in her mind. 'It was terrible to see all the items that belonged to the dead.'

The final list of survivors would consist of Joan, the driver's wife, a 17-year-old girl who had lost her mother, and a handful of pensioners who had been lucky.

Within the next few days, several of those who initially survived the crash would succumb to their injuries. The final death toll would be thirty-three, with a further thirteen injured, making this the worst-ever road accident in the United Kingdom, which it still is today.

The wrecked coach was hooked up to a large crane, slowly raised from its position and gently swung on to a flatbed lorry. The rest of the loose wreckage was placed on the back of a second lorry and together they made their way up the hill. The sight of such a sad cargo being escorted through the country roads was one that did not fit right with the surroundings, looking as out of place as any image could. The short journey ended at a Pateley Bridge garage, where the wreckage was propped up on stands for the investigators to go over.

A memorial service was held for the victims and survivors at Thornaby Methodist Church on 11 June and nearly 1,000 people attended. Messages of sympathy flooded in, including ones from the Queen, the Minister for Transport and the Prime Minister.

Led by the driver's final words before he died, along with the survivors' accounts of the coach picking up speed and not slowing as it approached the bend, investigators focused their attention on the braking system. At the inquest, which opened just a week after the crash, it was announced they had found that the rear offside brake had been completely inoperative, with neither the hand nor foot brakes being any use. A displaced roller in the brake expander unit was jammed, resulting in no movement of the brake shoes. Investigators found there was no wear on the brakes as they were not in contact with the drum. Another driver for Riley's told the inquest he had not been happy with the brakes on this coach and had stopped it on occasion, but he had taken it to Blackpool the day before the disaster and not found any problems with it. The inquest jury returned a verdict of accidental death.

On 5 November 1975 the coach owner, Norman Riley, pleaded guilty to using a motor vehicle on which the braking system was not properly maintained and adjusted. As he was not aware of the defects with the brakes, the magistrates did not revoke his licence and this allowed the company to continue operations. Instead he was fined £75.

The survivors of the disaster had to rebuild their lives and cope with whatever injuries they had. In some cases they would never recover from the mental scars, while others would take every opportunity to carry on with their lives. Just a year after the crash, two of the survivors went on a coach trip organised by the Teesside Senior Citizens Club using the same coach company; their determination not to let this disaster stop them living their lives made the headlines a few days after the first anniversary.

On 31 March 1976 a memorial plaque was unveiled by the Mayor of Stockton-on-Tees at the entrance to the Pavillion shopping precinct in the centre of Thornaby known as The Pavilion. This brass plaque did not list the victims but it did pay tribute to those who died. The three boys who were first on the scene of the crash were presented with an award for their outstanding assistance to those injured.

Today a second memorial stands outside Irene Jessop Funeral Service on Lanehouse Road in Thornaby listing all thirty-three names. Thornaby Town Council is planning a third memorial in the street outside the town hall, again listing the names of those killed.

Kevin Hullah stayed with Northallerton traffic division for another three years before he moved to CID and was sent to Scarborough, and then the regional crime squad in York. During a police career lasting thirty years, he would work on the investigation into the murder of Police Sergeant John Speed in Leeds in 1986 before retiring on New Year's Eve 2000. He would always say that the most memorable and largest job he ever did was the Dibbles Bridge disaster.

Basil Cardus sold his house in 1980 and moved to Skipton. Although he was not asked to give a statement by crash investigators, a few newspaper reporters spoke to him and his role in the rescue began to become part of history. Remembering his initial shock at seeing the dust cloud, he recalls, 'We've had one or two shocks before but that was the worst one.'

Although the Dibbles Bridge disaster is still the worst road crash in Britain, few people knew about it until Derek Smith and the local council made a well-researched documentary film detailing the events of that day. Featuring interviews with the survivors, witnesses and rescuers, it once again highlighted the tragic loss of life and the campaign for the public memorial. *Britain's Worst Road Disaster* premiered on Together TV in March 2019.

Today the roads leading to Dibbles Bridge feature signs warning of the 16 per cent gradient leading down to the bend in the road. There is nothing on the site or the house next to the bridge to say what happened here. As the years went on from the crash in 1975 and the parapet was rebuilt yet again, further tragedy was to come.

In 1986 a truck loaded with pine roof trusses crashed through the wall and landed upside down, mimicking the two coach disasters, and at least one cyclist has failed to stop and gone over the top. As the deaths continue to rise, we have to ask ourselves if enough is being done to stop these tragedies. The two coach accidents we know were due to brake failure, but what if chicanes, speed bumps or stronger collision barriers were put in place that would take the weight of a bus full of people, and if not stop the crash, then at least slow it down to a survivable level?

As we approach the centenary of the first coach crash, it seems that, other than a few road signs, very little has been done. It could be only a matter of time before the name Dibbles Bridge is once again back in the headlines.

16

1976: Fire on HMS *Glasgow*

The Royal Navy has always been one step ahead of the game when ships become old, with a programme in place to replace the old vessels by building them well in advance. The Navy gave the go-ahead for fourteen Type 42 destroyers to be built at four separate locations around the UK: Barrow, Newcastle, Birkenhead and Southampton. Named after major cities, they would be of 3,500 tons and the Batch 1 design would be 392ft long with a beam of 47ft. Others would follow, but the fourth ship of this class would be named after the city of Glasgow.

Built at by Swan Hunter in Newcastle upon Tyne, she was launched on 14 April 1976 and taken to the Neptune Yard to be fitted out alongside. Here the dockyard and construction workers would be back on board to install everything the ship would require to be a formidable fighting unit. She would be armed with a 4.5in gun at the bow as well as Sea Dart surface-to-air missiles on forward launchers and torpedo tubes, and would have the ability to carry a Lynx helicopter in her hangar.

On the early morning of Thursday, 23 September 1976, the ship was being prepared for another day of work, the night shift being relieved during a continuous, round-the-clock race to get the ship

HMS *Glasgow* in Portsmouth, 2008. During her build in 1976 a fire killed eight dockyard workers. (Author)

finished. At 07:35 most of the morning workforce were on board and ready to start, including a number of workers who descended into the auxiliary machinery space. Several of these started to light cigarettes, as being able to smoke below decks was not unusual for those days. But something strange happened that none of them could understand. When the lighters were lit they emitted a whitish flame, and when the cigarette was lit it burned away extremely rapidly. Nobody realised that these were signs of an oxygen-enriched atmosphere, a situation that could have very dangerous results.

At around 07:55 a welder was at work close to the door to the compartment when he struck an arc (started a weld, a bit like striking a match) and found that the glow was not its usual colour – white instead of blue. Suddenly the cables hanging down nearby caught fire and the fire spread so quickly it was impossible to just pat it out with his hands. The fire flashed up and down the compartment along the cables and several of the men down there realised that a serious fire had suddenly broken out. They started to evacuate the compartment but only four of them managed to get out. By now the section was fully ablaze with thick black smoke emitting through the escape route.

Apprentice electrician Denis Pratt was working in the aft end of the ship. He had only left school the previous year, determined to find a job as an electrical apprentice, but his initial attempts were unsuccessful:

One of the interviews was at Swan Hunters for the electrical apprentice role. Sadly, I wasn't offered it but they did offer me a role as an apprentice welder, which I turned down. On reflection, turning up thirty minutes late because I had been queuing for concert tickets at the City Hall probably didn't help, but at that age you have different priorities.

Once I left school, I received my exam results, which were better than the school had predicted, and the local career advice service called me in to offer me a chance to train as an electrical apprentice at Hebburn Technical College training. This was a year-long course but offered to find a permanent industrial placement to finish the apprenticeship within this first year. As they had indicated as the year progressed, we were asked to attend interviews with local businesses and I remember being asked to attend an interview at Swan Hunters midway through the first year. To my surprise I was offered an apprenticeship, this time in my chosen electrical trade.

My First Year at Swan's was based in the training school not far from the bone yard and pickle factory opposite the Neptune shipyard, fortunately far enough away for us not to notice the pungent aroma of the combined stench.

Having spent time in this training school learning the basics and meeting new friends, we were all allocated a shipyard within the Swan Hunter Group for our second year starting after the summer break. I was allocated Neptune shipyard, and the main entrance was far closer to the previously mentioned bone yard and pickle factory. I remember my first few days experiencing this in its full summer glory, not something I would recommend.

As a 17-year-old I started work at the Neptune yard early in August 1976, with the first days in work being very daunting as I was assigned to my journeyman and shown to my work area on board HMS *Glasgow* for the first time. I remember looking in at HMS *Newcastle* just ahead of *Glasgow* thinking this was one of the finest Navy ships I had ever been close to, whereas *Glasgow* was not looking as refined as it was still mostly painted with a red primer and had lots of weld scars on its outer hull. As I slowly settled into my new work environment I found some of the traditions (pranks) played by my journeymen and his peers continued as part of my training experience. At the time, though these were at my expense and mostly harmless, I didn't understand the risky environment we were in.

That morning Denis had taken his usual journey to work, getting on the bus under the flyover at the Robin Hood bus stop half asleep, then running for the ferry at Hebburn, jumping on it as it pulled away. Arriving at the dockyard, he went on board the *Glasgow* as usual and looked at the progress that had been made since he first came on board:

I do remember that during the build the conversion machinery room, which was located on the lower deck of the vessel, had a shipping hole left out of the hull to allow the heavy machinery to be lowered into place and was just aft of the single forward gangway that we used to get on and off the vessel. This wasn't an issue normally as we all knew it was there and it was clearly visible. Once on board, I now remember I was in an electrical distribution room adjacent to the aft switchboard room working with my journeyman, Ronny. We were just starting our daily tasks when suddenly there were whistles being blown on board the boat and for some obscure reason we were mostly ignoring it. After a few short minutes, one of the foremen on board put his head into the room and shouted, 'Why are you still here? You need to evacuate now!'

Shocked into reality, Denis and his team got up and headed out. This is where it all became real and, from it being a normal day, it quickly became chaotic and confusing:

I tried to exit the ship by my normal route and realised two-deck passageway was thick with smoke, making the route impossible to use. Fortunately, as we were quite far aft we were well away from the fire at the forward end of the ship and I quickly made my way up to the open deck aft. I then joined the queue of people that had formed making their way to the single exit at the forward end of the ship. I could now clearly see the dark acrid smoke billowing out of the removed section of deck above the conversion machinery room and suddenly became very aware of this hole in the deck, which was no longer visible. I eventually took my turn in traversing through the blanket of smoke, tightly following the handrail until I found the opening to the gangway. Still through thick black smoke, I continued down the gangway and at about midway I started to struggle to stay conscious as the smoke was suffocating me. It was then I remember a fireman grabbing me towards the end and helping me off the gangway to a point where I could once again see and, more importantly, breathe. I don't remember much of what went on within the shipyard after that point but I would guess they recorded all those who were fortunate to get off the vessel.

Kenneth Hyland was another welder working on board that day and he and his mates were having a cup of tea in the hangar area. He had been working on constructing the cabin assembly and, when the fire alarm went off, he and his workmates made their way through the ship towards the forward section to get off via the single gangway. In all the confusion, some of the lads headed to the smoke-filled compartments; Kenneth and his workmates had to shout after them to get out while they could.

Twenty-one-year-old electrician Alexander Crawford had clocked on as normal at 07:30 and he too went for a cup of tea with his workmates, Swifty and Micky, over in the junior rates' mess. They had a bit of time before the gaffers came on board and were enjoying their brew. Alexander had only been married two months and had started his job as an apprentice when he was just 16 years old, finding the workforce a close-knit bunch and enjoying his chance to follow his father into the shipbuilding industry. Suddenly a head appeared at the hatch. 'Everyone ashore, there's a fire!' he said. That was good news … a bit of time to get off the ship and skive off work, he thought.

Gathering up their gear, they climbed out of the hatch and went forward towards the gangway, but suddenly the lights went out. This was serious – there were obstacles all over the place and now they had to feel their way down the ship from below the waterline right up to fresh air. As it was pitch black, they were banging their heads constantly and tripping over things until they realised they had reached the cross passage where you could go either way. People were coming from the right and saying that they couldn't get out that way, while others were now pushing each other in their haste to figure out where they were going and to get out of the dark void that the *Glasgow* had become. What made it worse for them now was the smell of smoke that was hitting their nostrils and going into their lungs. He continued:

We head up the port side as we know there was a ladder going up around midships. We are feeling our way along but not really panicking. We bump into people coming aft looking for the same ladder, jostling to go up when those above started coming back down. The smoke is getting thicker and its starting to get scary. 'The smoke's too thick up there go forward,' someone shouts. So away we go, we reach the ladder and can see daylight and fresh air. 'Get ashore! Get ashore! Wait for a card check,' the gaffers are shouting.

Alexander and his mates were the lucky ones; the ship was now filling with smoke and several people were unaccounted for. The fire brigade were quick in getting to the ship and they were straight on board with breathing apparatus. The first thing they did was step on 'Big Alan', a welder, who was unconscious at the bottom of a ladder. They dragged him off the ship and rushed him to the ambulance room. In the meantime, the names of the lads were called out to check who was still there. There was silence between the men; there was nothing much to say but watch the spectacle of the blaze being tackled by the firefighters from the inside.

The ladders inside were made of wood so the fire crews had to use ropes to get to the scene of the fire. The first body was located and recovered; blankets were requested to cover it up as it came ashore. Tied only with a rope around the middle, the wind blew the corner of the blanket and revealed the face of Peter Dowie, a friend Alexander went to training school with. 'He looked like he was asleep,' he recalled forty-four years later.

In the chaos of the disaster, the men were checked off the list and sent home. However, Alexander forgot one important thing:

I rang my new wife and told her I was OK but forgot to let my father know. He was in the next yard, up river in the Naval Yard.

He knew I was on the *Glasgow*, so came down to see if I was safe but when he asked about me the manager in charge asked if I had any tattoos or distinguishing marks to identify me by. My father thought there were a lot of fatalities so decided to come to my new flat to put his mind at rest and gave me one hell of a bollocking for not letting him know.

One of the firefighters on the *Glasgow* that morning was Tom Lyall. Working from Gateshead station, he had only been a member of Tyne and Wear Metropolitan Fire Brigade since February 1975 and now, aged just 21, he was here tackling a difficult fire:

We waited a while up on deck, then went down into the area where the main spread of fire was. I can't really remember if the light was OK or if we needed extra illumination but I still have a fairly vivid image of where most of the bodies were discovered, certainly one main area where the three that my boss located when he led the team before us. I can remember that a press helicopter was continually hovering over the vessel and I remember a senior police officer telling a constable to get its number!

The fire team was there until at least the early afternoon. They had to carry out a number of searches as the roll-call carried out on the jetty was incomplete. Several people had clocked on to their shift and then left the vessel, so it was difficult to tell if these were actually casualties.

Thirty-three-year-old Leonard Henry was captain of the first air rescue team, and he was already tired after spending the previous day travelling to and from London for a competition that saw him back in the North-East in the early hours of the morning. He had worked at the shipyard all his adult life and his father had died there, which had inspired him to work towards making the dockyard safer for others.

At around 07:50 he arrived late for work after missing the bus; he normally started at half past. As he went into the office to clock on, the time office lad looked at him and said, 'Len, you better get down to the ship, there's problems on it!'

'Which ship?'

'The *Glasgow*,' he replied.

That was strange – he was working on the *Newcastle* not the *Glasgow*, what did this have to do with him? Either way it sounded serious, so it may need his first-aid expertise. As he made his way to the ship he saw a scene of chaos with people everywhere. 'What's happened?' he asked.

'There's been an explosion,' someone replied.

Lenny was confused, as the ship looked fine from the outside and it didn't seem as if there were any blast holes. But the fire brigade were already retrieving bodies by this point. The fire teams needed help finding their way around the ship; it was purgatory in there, trying to recover the victims, and so Lenny was asked to describe to the fire teams the best routes in and out and what to avoid, getting them to the upper deck as quickly as they could. They soon located several bodies where Lenny had told them to go, but water that had been used to put out the fires was now beginning to fill some of the compartments. Lenny warned the firefighters to turn off their hoses or the ship would become unstable.

On board the blackened ship it was a labyrinth of hazards, and once Lenny got on to two-deck he was in pitch darkness, the power having been cut earlier on. He led the firefighters further below, and because it was a strange direction they questioned where he was taking them.

It did not take long for the awful truth of the scale of the disaster to become apparent. Eight people were dead and several more were in hospital suffering from smoke inhalation. The bodies of the deceased were found on three- and four-decks in G section, their place of work. One of the bodies was found in a cupboard, where the victim had tried to escape the fire and smoke.

Alexander Crawford remembers the mood in the dockyard still being sombre a few days later when a second incident occurred:

A few days after the fire, a worker fell off the back of HMS *Newcastle*, which was moored in front of *Glasgow*. He landed on a wooden raft used to stop the ship bumping into the jetty. He was unconscious but half in and half out of the water. They lowered a rescue cage down to him and the safety officer (Lenny Henry) got hold of the back of his coat but not a good hold and put his hand up to tell the crane driver to stop, but the crane driver, thinking it was the signal to lift (a winding motion with the hand), started lifting. He lost his grip on the man's coat and he slipped off the raft and went under the water. His body was recovered a few days later down river. I think it was on or the day before his 27th birthday.

A post-mortem examination revealed the injury sustained in the initial fall was what killed him.

Denis Pratt left the dockyard the day of the fire with a bitter contempt for the press who were attempting to get a story while the rescue operations were going on; he viewed them as getting in the way of the emergency services. He headed home and then met up with his girlfriend (now wife) and completely forgot about telling his mother what had gone on: 'While I was clearly OK and discussing what had just happened with my girlfriend I had completely forgotten my mother, who was at work at the time, had heard all of this unfold on the radio and had no idea if I had made it off the ship alive and she had feared the worst.'

Denis's work as an electrical apprentice only continued for another few months before he found himself in the drawing office as an apprentice electrical draughtsman:

Within months of this I had moved on to the commissioning team, and I returned to HMS *Glasgow* and commissioned the very switchboards I had helped build as a very green electrical apprentice. I remained in the commissioning role throughout the remainder of my career and had the pleasure of taking many other Swan Hunter vessels including two aircraft carriers and HMS *York* (a stretched Type 42) to sea as the commissioning manager responsible for the team operating all the machinery on board throughout sea trials. I remained in that role until the shipyard closed and then Joined VSEL, initially commissioning the surface ships HMS *Ocean* and HMS *Albion* but more recently commissioning and on the sea trials of three of the Astute-class submarines.

Lenny Henry, the first-aid captain and later safety officer, would go on to receive the MBE and a medal for bravery for his work in the dockyard. For many years after he would train fire teams and others in how to remove casualties from ships and draw up plans for scenarios that have been used ever since, including arrangements for an incident command post where personnel were to meet in the event of an emergency.

The investigation into the fire on board the *Glasgow* found that an oxygen hose had been leaking slightly due to a tap being left on from the previous day. The slow release of oxygen had filled the compartments and made them a ticking time bomb for when the welders came on board and lit their torches. The incident is today used as a real-life scenario for training in health and safety at BAE Systems and various other organisations.

The *Glasgow* was eventually repaired and work continued to bring the ship up to standard for the official handover to the Royal Navy. In a ceremony held in her home port of Portsmouth, she was officially commissioned into the fleet on Friday, 9 March 1979. She saw action in the South Atlantic during the Falklands conflict, when an unexploded bomb crashed through her hull and out the other side. The miracle escape from certain death was a testament to her crew, as the holes were quickly patched up and she lived to fight another day.

The *Glasgow*, with her pennant number D88 emblazoned across her hull, served the fleet for twenty-six years until she was decommissioned in February 2005. Four years later she was towed out of Portsmouth Harbour bound for a Turkish scrapyard. So ended the career of one of the modern Royal Navy's best-loved warships.

17

1980: Denmark Place Arson Attack

Denmark Place in London has always been famous for the comings and goings of people in the music industry. Back to back with Denmark Street, in the 1960s it would not be unknown to see the likes of David Bowie, the Rolling Stones and Elton John recording songs in the studios above the shops selling the latest records and instruments.

However, the upper floors of these buildings had little to do with the glamour of the rich and famous. In one building, No. 18 Denmark Place, two illegal nightclubs thrived – El Hueco (aka the Spanish Rooms) and the South American club Rodo's. Together these were simply known as 'Dandy's'. These unlicensed venues operated in secrecy and were a regular haunt for many an immigrant who wanted a taste of back home or who simply wanted to be left alone.

These were not clubs that you could simply walk into; you had to attract attention from the street below in order to be let in. The clubs were known to the police and a plan was put in place to shut them down

On the early morning of Saturday, 16 August 1980, a 42-year-old Scot named John Thompson was in the Spanish Rooms

Redevelopment of Denmark Place area in 2015. (Author)

drinking away the night. He was known by many nicknames, including 'The Gypsy' and 'Punch', and had been at other venues that night before he had decided to come to Denmark Place. Asking for another drink, his aggressive side soon came out when he got into an argument with the bartender. He had already had too much to drink and it is possible his quarrel was to do with his belief that he was being overcharged for his drink. Either way, the bar staff did not want trouble like Thompson and he was thrown out into the street, with the door locked behind him. Thompson was furious, and as he walked away from the club, he found a 2-gallon can nearby. He picked it up and hailed a taxi driven by a Mr Dawar, being heard to say he was going to 'sort them out' and pointing back to the club. Mr Dawar took him to a petrol station in Camden, where he bought a gallon of fuel. Thompson then returned to Denmark Place to seek his revenge.

At around 03:30 that morning, he walked up to the letterbox of No. 18 and poured the contents of the can through. He then lit a piece of paper, posted it through and made his escape.

The petrol lit straight away and what was shocking was the speed at which this fire took hold. Flames raced up the staircase and cut off any chances of escape by the people in the clubs. Boarded-up windows and locked doors prevented anybody getting out and some had to smash windows as the smoke billowed into the rooms. Several jumped from a great height on to the building backing on to the club, while others found themselves with no option but to try to climb down.

The wooden staircase fuelled the flames and before too long the fire had reached the upper floors. Many of the occupants had not even time to leave their seats, the smoke and flames knocking them unconscious in seconds, and they died where they sat.

The street where this was all happening was on the Soho area fire brigade's patch and they were first to be called out, soon followed by Euston and Manchester Square teams.

The scene following the fire at Denmark Place, London, which resulted in the deaths of thirty-seven people. (Courtesy Mirrorpix/Reach Licensing)

The Soho brigade were on the scene very quickly but all they could do was rescue the people clinging to the outside of the building and from the music shop opposite, where they had become trapped by a security shutter. Fire teams took four minutes to break down the front door of No. 16 and they immediately saw the entire staircase was a raging inferno.

Thirty-four-year-old firefighter Dave Pare had been part of London's fire teams since joining in 1966 and had already had a fair few big jobs in his time, including dealing with IRA bombs and a parcel bomb at the Israeli Embassy in the 1970s. When the call came into his station at Euston saying there was a fire at Denmark Place, he didn't even know where that was. He had been up and down the main Tottenham Court Road hundreds of times but had never noticed Denmark Place before, and certainly didn't know there were hidden nightclubs up there. The fire engines left the station at the corner of Euston Road and Eversholt Street and sped to the scene down Tottenham Court Road. They parked on Denmark Place itself but could not see anything. However, as he made his way around the corner, Dave saw what looked like a riot. People were running around all over the place and screaming.

He saw that some of the club-goers had managed to get out of the window. His colleague 'Aggie' Weston saw the Soho station officer nearby and they agreed that Soho would take the front door and Euston the back, attacking the fire from both sides. Dave and his team were at the music shop on Denmark Street when he saw a survivor inside trying to smash his way out through the glass and via the security grille that was still in place. The survivor was shouting over and over again, 'There's hundreds dead!' as he was rescued and was taken away with injuries on his arms and wrists where he had cut himself trying to escape.

Incredibly there were still no flames visible from where Dave was standing, so he and his colleagues slowly made their way up the broken building from the outside. A window had been smashed and the curtains were blowing out of the kitchen area. The back fire escape was still usable and he made his way up with his team and saw the staircase going directly down to the ground floor. Soho would be dealing with the fire on the second floor, and Euston would sort out the first floor before moving up.

As he made his way up to the kitchen area Dave saw three bodies. This was the location where the survivor he had found had been, before he had escaped via the fire escape at the back and had got across a little courtyard and through the music shop. It was now clear to Dave how the man had got out, but he was the only survivor he had seen so far.

Dave had a number of tasks to perform: primarily searching the flats opposite the fire escapes as the explosion had blown out windows above the music shop and they had to make sure no fire had spread here – thankfully there was no further fire and no casualties, so he came out.

As the firemen reached the top floor it became obvious that the fire had shot up very quickly had pretty much blown the roof off, as the petrol had ignited at the bottom and most likely mixed with everything flammable in the bar. The staircase had created a blast route and the resulting flames had obliterated anything in their path.

In the aftermath there were people laid out dead on the main roads, which left a lot of people not even realising that there had been a fire at first. The roof was a complete skeleton, blackened and smouldering, with smoke still rising into the air as the dawn light showed a charred building with barely anything recognisable inside.

When the lifesaving work had been done, the fire engines were soon removed to be available for other callouts, and Dave was not on scene for long. 'It was not difficult getting up to the fire. In through the shop, through the fire escape, knock the fire out, dampen down. No real hard work.' (I suspect he is being modest at this point.)

Homerton Fire Station crews then came to relieve them. 'Follow our hose up to the fire,' they were told. 'There's twenty-seven found dead.'

The fireman must have thought he was just joking around. 'You f★★king A division blokes are always bigging it up,' he replied.

But the Homerton crew went up and were shocked at what greeted them. The report held was no word of a lie and the fireman immediately apologised for his comments with the words, 'It's now gone up to thirty-two,' after counting several more bodies.

By now the other teams had to conduct the removal of the victims and allow the police photographers to do their work, as well as allow investigators to look for evidence of what had caused the fire. From what they could see, this was clearly an arson attack.

Looking around at the burned rooms, victims were still sat at their tables where they died instantly, playing cards or drinking. Dave remembers them looking unreal, 'like tailor's dummies'. He stayed on the first floor and did not venture up any further to where the others bodies were located.

As the fire teams sifted through the burned wreckage of the building, cooling down the last of the hot spots, it soon became apparent that there were dozens of bodies strewn all around the place. By the time they had completed their firefighting, there was a shocking total of thirty-seven dead.

Police had to start from scratch. The owner of the building was on holiday in Europe, so he would be no use at the moment. Forensics had taken away a small container found nearby that may have contained a flammable substance. Considering all the signs pointed to the fire starting at the bottom of the stairs, arson was looking more and more likely. Due to the nature of the clubs, rumours were rife about the perpetrator being a drug lord, a gangster or one of a number of rival dealers in the area out to make their mark.

But eyewitnesses started to come forward suggesting a man who had been refused entry after being kicked out of the club.

Within days a team of more than thirty detectives had formed a murder squad to track down the killer. A photo composite impression of a suspect sporting dark sunglasses and a large moustache and carrying a petrol can was distributed to potential witnesses. However, those who drank there that night were reluctant to come forward with information, and the police were finding it very difficult to speak to those who may or may not be able to identify the killer.

However, they soon had their man. John Thompson was arrested and charged with a single murder, that of Archibald Campbell, as well as this arson attack and another similar one earlier in the year at a flat. He pleaded not guilty.

Thompson's trial began in April 1981, where incredibly he not only denied the attack but claimed that he had bought the petrol and put it down in Denmark Place while he went to look for a battery to steal for his car.

Despite his claims, on 7 May a jury found Thompson guilty of the murder of Archibald Campbell and of arson at Denmark Place. He was found not guilty of the previous attack at the Hackney apartment. On 17 June the coroner announced all the victims had died as a result of smoke inhalation.

In one final twist to this story, the killer died of cancer on the twenty-eighth anniversary of the fire. His death was barely noticed and hardly reported.

Euston firefighter Dave Pare had a long career with the London Fire Brigade. A few years after this fire he became an instructor on breathing apparatus, giving lectures on other major disasters in the London area such as the 1987 King's Cross fire and the 1975 Moorgate Tube crash. He retired in 1996 after thirty years of service.

What is incredible about this huge loss of life is that it really is one of Britain's worst forgotten disasters. The largest act of non-terrorist-related mass murder in the United Kingdom until Harold Shipman was arrested in 1998 was front-page news the morning after the fire. However, the arrest of the killer and his trial occupied such a small space in the newspapers that it would have been missed if you didn't search for it specifically.

How could this be? Well, first of all, Thompson's trial was going on at the same time as that of the Yorkshire Ripper, Peter Sutcliffe, and both were being held at the Old Bailey. As he was being found guilty and jailed, the papers were more interested in the sensational details of the Ripper's reign of terror, which seemed to sell more papers than the story of a grumpy drunken Scotsman who firebombed a bunch of immigrants. If the news-papers had investigated this story a little more they would have found dozens of stories, a trial worth talking about and the chance to remember those who died. The problem was that the press just didn't care.

For the families of the thirty-seven victims, their lives have been blighted by this horrific event, yet so little is written about it even today.

The building where this attack happened has, within the last few years, been demolished as part of a redevelopment scheme. Despite calls in news articles that are published here and there over the decades, there is no memorial to one of the worst acts of mass murder Britain has ever seen.

18

1981: New Cross Fire

Just five months after the Denmark Place arson attack, London was shocked by a second fire that took more than a dozen lives, only this time it was surrounded by far more controversy.

New Cross Road in South London was a long stretch of main street in a neighbourhood of Black families. No. 439 was one of a number of large terraced houses that towered three storeys high. On the evening of 17 January 1981, the residents there decided to hold a party to celebrate the birthday of two young people – one turning 16, the other 18.

As guests arrived, the house soon filled up with young revellers who were either friends or relatives of the hosts, and things were going great as the music blared into the night. As with any party, especially when people consume too much alcohol, confrontations break out. Two of the lads were arguing over dancing with a girl and it looked like it was going to get physical at one point, until things naturally calmed down. Other people would later claim that a fight did occur within the house.

In the early hours of the following morning, the party was still going strong. Dawn was not far away and by now those who had partied all night were growing tired. At the height of the celebrations there were up to 200 people there but now it was estimated it was down to sixty to eighty. At around 05:30 that morning a flammable liquid was released on to the carpet in the front room and set alight. The room was on fire very quickly and incredibly the people inside did not know what was amiss at first.

A passing motorist saw the flames and tried to get the attention of those inside and tell them their house was on fire. Having no luck, he raced to the nearest police station and raised the alarm. The room itself had been placed out of bounds by the owner, so nobody would have known what was going on, that is until the smoke started billowing out and heading up the stairs.

The fire took hold quickly and the partygoers soon found themselves trapped by smoke and flames. By now the call was out and the London Fire Brigade were on their way.

Firefighter John Taylor was aged 18 and had only been out of training for two months. His team at Deptford was the first on the scene. John was on the night shift when the alarms went off at 05:45 with multiple calls. Both units at that station were sent out and he was sat in the truck looking out of the window, speeding towards what was to be his first big fire.

As the engine pulled up at the scene, John looked out of his window and saw every floor ablaze except the first, for some reason. Because he had only been out of training two months, he could not wear breathing apparatus (he needed six months' experience), so he was given priority messages to send instead. The first one was an update that four pumps had arrived (three initial response and Deptford as an addition) to ask for ambulances to be despatched.

Despite the large number of people now wandering around the street, a team from Greenwich allowed him to use their radio right outside the front door to relay the messages back to control.

The chaos was constant – a girl was lying on the pavement in front of the fire engines being given first aid as blood was pouring from the back of her head where she had jumped from a window to escape. Another man had jumped from a window and had accidentally ended up falling into the basement. Despite suffering multiple broken bones, he was still alive. Another man whose shirt was covered in blood was helped away by police for medical attention.

The Deptford truck was then taken around the back of the building where, due to the house being on an incline, there were actually four floors. A fence had to be broken down in order to get to the rear, where survivors were now laid out in the yard needing medical attention. They had all tried to climb down the drain-pipe but it had collapsed under their weight and they had all fallen down together.

John had now been on scene for an hour and was feeding hoses up the escape at the front. Once the smoke had cleared enough he was allowed to go in himself.

By now one crew was spraying the building on the outside, while others had made an entry from the front and were making their way through the rooms inside. Eight people were found in the front room, four of whom were still alive, and they were taken away.

The top floor was a mess. The roof had collapsed and the land-ing was unsafe. Four badly burned bodies were piled up in one room, three of them under a window and another leaning out of the window with arms in the air. Fire crews found who they sus-pected was the DJ in the front bedroom at the top left of the stairs, buried under the wreckage of the roof. He had apparently initially managed to get out but returned to save his records or belongings.

The police had been trying to cordon off the street from onlookers but there were still people running around and scream-ing, some being led away to receive first aid and then taken away to hospital in vans. Flaming embers were still falling out of the window and on to the street below, potentially on to the people still there. The whole area around 439 New Cross Road had been closed by then to all people not involved in the firefighting and rescue efforts.

It was around 09:30 when John and his team were relieved. By then the fire crews were just damping down and covering the bodies up as best they could. They had been trying to cover the victim who was still leaning out the top-floor window at the back, but the sheet kept catching fire as the window frames were smouldering. They were not allowed to move the body yet as it had to be left in situ for the coroner. The people down below in the street could see it, so it had to be covered up somehow, which they did in the end, but fire teams had to carry on spraying it with water to prevent it from bursting into flames again.

After an exhausting morning, the rest of the crew assured John that this was not a normal day and a job like this did not come around often. For that he could be thankful at least.

Arthur 'Tug' Wilson was a firefighter still under training when word came out that a building was on fire on New Cross Road. He had joined London Fire Brigade fewer than three months ago and he had spent a lot of time at the training centre at Southwark Fire Station. After each week of training you moved up a squad and this week he would be attending the New Cross incident.

When the call came in, the station officer drove a crew bus with around twelve firefighters down to the scene, but when they arrived the sight of the disaster stopped them in their tracks. The full horror of the crowd of young people traumatised and looking for their missing friends was something that Tug would never forget. Two fire engines were parked outside making best use of the space available on the roadside. They had already rigged ladders inside and were hard at work within the confined and blackened rooms.

The team went into the building and, as by now most of the bodies had already been taken away, they were tasked to go into the

The site of the New Cross fire today with the plaque placed in memory of the victims. (Author)

rooms and shift the debris to make sure nothing was left behind that should not be. As it was officially a crime scene, they had to be careful not to touch anything that may be evidence. Steam and water was everywhere, and the smell was almost like a barbecue; they tried not to think too much about what had gone on there. The roof and the flooring inside was mostly gone, and the other crews were pointing out areas of interest to them while they stayed out of the way of those who had a job to do. Being a trainee meant keeping out of the way but learning as much as possible on site. After about thirty minutes in the house, the team reassembled and was sent back to the training school for a debrief.

George Thompson, 28, had only just finished his training after joining London Fire Brigade the previous August. He had completed it in December and was now in Green Watch at Southwick station, next door to the training centre. He was normally on call day and night, with only one day off in two weeks.

At 08:30 that morning George had arrived at the station to start his 09:00 day shift and the talk of the teams was the job over at New Cross. He would ride on one of the relief pump escape ladders with the rest of his team and, as they got to the burned house, he realised something very quickly – he had never seen dead bodies before, and this would be his first time. Nothing prepared him for the sight that greeted him when he entered No. 439.

'The smell was dreadful, the fire was out but it was still very hot,' he recalls. The ceiling had come down along with some of the joists, while the three floors and attic were all gutted beyond recognition. A ladder had to be put up as the stairs were either completely gone or unsafe to use. The police were there, along with the forensics teams trying to figure out what had gone on here overnight to have caused such a horrific blaze.

George made his way to the second floor, where he saw a lot of bodies. Several were at the back of the building, and it looked as if the victims had been trying to get out of the window when they had died. Because of the enormity of the task, and the fact they had to be careful in such an unstable environment, the fire teams were stood outside out of the way until they were called in to do a specific job. This included moving the ladders around and bringing coffins in and out to remove the bodies.

The scene inside was not one that George cared to spend any more time in than he had to. 'All you could see was burnt brick, the plaster had all come off the walls, furniture burned down to just the metal pieces like the springs in the sofa.'

The coffins were carried in for the bodies to be taken away by the coroner, and many victims were burned beyond recognition.

By now many people had turned up to see the scene, and a cordon was in place to keep the public back. By midday George's job was done and he was heading back to the station. What struck him was the fact that none of the neighbours had brought out refreshments to the fire teams like they did on other jobs. Normally they were inundated with cups of tea, but in this case nothing. By the time George got back he was famished and his first priority was to seek out some lunch.

That night George told his wife about the things he had seen; he was upset, thinking about the victims of a tragedy that should never have happened. In those days the act of talking about something traumatic in order to process it was something that might easily have been laughed at. PTSD was not even thought about for rescue teams in the 1980s, but thankfully he was able to talk about it all. He went on to spend just under thirty years in the Fire Brigade, including attending the 1987 fire at King's Cross Station that killed thirty-one people including a fire officer.

The fire at New Cross Road was now being treated as arson. There were clear signs that an accelerant had been used and the forensics teams were finding evidence that several partygoers had been fighting. As so many statements were taken and then retracted, it was difficult for the police to find a substantial amount of evidence that the cause of the fire was arson and not a simple accident.

By the evening it was reported that there was animosity in the community, with some people saying the rescue services had not done enough, but this was a false report as a later meeting with the Black community confirmed that they were happy that everything had been done to help the best they could.

When the final count was made official, thirteen people were listed as being killed in the fire and, in a tragic final twist, another person committed suicide a year later after being traumatised by the events.

The fire not only destroyed lives but it heightened tensions between the Black community and the authorities. Marches took place calling it the 'New Cross Massacre' and claiming that the deaths were the result of a racially motivated attack. When the inquests were opened and evidence heard in court, the coroner, Arthur Davies, had to contend with a constant flow of statements that were then retracted. Family members shouted across the court and the public were threatened with exclusion if there were any more interruptions.

On 13 May 1981 an open verdict was returned on the thirteen victims, the jury undecided on the evidence over whether the cause was deliberate or accidental. The families of those killed called immediately for the verdict to be quashed and a new inquest launched.

Based on the evidence submitted, the seat of the fire was the centre of the front room. If it had been a fire bomb through the window, as many people claimed, it would not have gone that far into the room and therefore was the least likely cause. With the case now closed, relatives screamed 'Murderers!' into the streets in the full glare of press photographers.

For more than twenty years campaigners fought vigorously for the inquest verdict to be quashed and in 1997 the police reopened the investigation. With five years of more vigorous interviews and rechecking evidence, in October 2002 the High Court agreed that a fresh inquest should look at the evidence.

On 6 May 2004, a Southwark Crown Court inquest led by Gerald Butler QC recorded open verdicts once again. He stated that, while he believed it was most likely the fire was caused by a deliberate act, there was simply not enough evidence to record a verdict of unlawful killing. Ten months later the families were refused leave to challenge the verdict, but the police were confident that, unless new evidence iswasfound and presented to a court, this would remain an arson attack by persons unknown, whether inside the house or not. However, until that happened it would be an open case for the police and another case of waiting for the families.

The one thing that is clear is that whatever happened that night, fourteen people are now dead, with many more having the images of what went on during that fire playing on repeat within their heads. With not enough evidence to say otherwise, the case has always been classed as unsolved. Until fresh evidence can be found, the families of those who died face a long wait for justice.

The house at 439 New Cross Road was repaired and still stands today. On the thirtieth anniversary of the fire in 2011, a plaque on the front wall was unveiled that remembers all fourteen who died as a result of the fire that is slowly fading from London's memory.

19

1984: Abbeystead Explosion

When a disaster occurs in a big city, it gets big headlines and major news coverage. However, when it happens in the middle of the countryside far from any major city, it is amazing just how quickly the event is lost from people's minds, until a time comes when nobody has even heard of the place you mention. For some small towns and villages, their names are forever linked with bigger tragedies – Lockerbie, Dunblane, Hungerford and Soham. But for the tiny village of Abbeystead in Lancashire, the name would become infamous for a short period of time, but the fallout from the tragedy would last a lot longer.

Classed as a small hamlet, Abbeystead is an area within the Forest of Bowland Area of Outstanding Natural Beauty and some of the few buildings there date back hundreds of years. Through the middle of this area run the two rivers Wyre and Lune, with a valve house built right in the middle where water could be transferred from one river or the other to meet any increase in demand from the residents, which had shown signs of needing further expansion by the early 1980s.

On 23 May 1984 thirty-eight people were attending a presentation by the North West Water Authority on the operational aspects of the station. A lot of residents believed that the pumping station working the rivers had led to flooding that had seriously affected the village of St Michael's on Wyre, which was around 10 miles away. The tour was intended to put minds at rest and prove that the pumping station was not the cause. At 19:20 that evening the guide started his tour and showed everybody the inspection chambers, which would be followed by a demonstration of the pumping procedure. This was meant to be a relaxed evening of reassurance that the operations were safe and not in any way connected to the flooding.

The NWWA district manager, George Lacey, called the River Lune pumping station to ask them to begin pumping water, but this was followed a few minutes later by another phone call to say that nothing had come through yet and that he should start the second larger pump.

Memorial plaque situated outside the valve house. (Simon Tebbutt)

What nobody realised was that the whole area was a coal bed and that any water going through the pipes had a quantity of methane gas mixing in. This had been building up over time and was getting to a point of no return – something that nobody had taken into account or expected. The party of visitors were not warned not to smoke, and it is thought that somebody may have lit a cigarette at the exact time the methane build-up hit the valve house. The result was devastating.

At approximately 19:30 a huge blast shook through the Abbeystead valve house and lifted the underground concrete roof high into the air, taking the topsoil and ground with it before it all fell back down into the chamber below.

Around a mile and half away lived Francis O'Neill. The 43-year-old doctor worked as both a GP and at hospitals, and on that day he was enjoying his time with his two children, aged 6 and 7, after his wife had left to play tennis over in Windermere. As her car was only a small one – a Mini – he agreed that she should take his car. It was a beautiful evening, with a warm, golden sunset that you only get during summers in the countryside.

Francis was in the house at the time and did not hear anything that was going on over at the valve house, his double-glazed windows making sure no noise got in that would disturb him. Suddenly a car came speeding up his drive and a woman shouted over to him that there had been an explosion at the pumping station and there were casualties. As a doctor, he needed to get there as soon as possible!

There was just one problem – his medical bag was in his car, which had been taken by his wife. So with no bag and a Mini to drive down in, he quickly knocked on his next-door neighbour's door and asked the two teenagers there to watch his children while he went to the scene, racing down the main road and turning off on the concrete track that led down to the valve house. As he approached the turning, though, he saw people stood around, and as he got closer he could see that they were injured; 'walking wounded' would have been the best way to describe them. He knew that if these people were here walking around, there would be people needing attention further towards the site. Their injuries were clearly burns to the exposed skin on their hands, arms and faces. He guessed that these were the lucky ones and that he was about to come upon people who were more seriously injured just a bit further on. If those he had seen were fit enough to walk this far then people could take them to hospital from here. He pressed on and headed further down the track.

As he approached the site of the blast he realised that he was the first person on the scene and, for a long time after, the only doctor. He pulled up and walked over to the remains of the station and was shocked by the sight that met him. Concrete pillars had been snapped like matchsticks and the rooms below were now exposed, grass and masonry covering the areas where it had fallen in on itself and caved in. Looking around, he saw people milling around, obviously suffering from burns. Local farmers arrived to help, but with no medical knowledge and lacking any medival equipment, all they could do was comfort the injured.

What struck Francis was the silence of the people. There was no wailing, weeping or screaming with terror. Nothing. It was still a peaceful evening with no noise or smoke from the aftermath and nobody rushing around in panic.

The emergency services had been called, but it would be a while yet before they arrived. Francis saw two cars parked nearby, the glass completely blown out of them by the explosion, but inside each car were four people who had sensibly decided to use the two vehicles as places to sit until help arrived. All eight occupants had serious burns and, despite the hot weather, were all shivering. Again, all Francis could do was reassure them and talk to them.

Nearby on a concrete shelf were two people, a man and a woman. One of them had a broken leg, while the other was sitting upright but was obviously dead. Francis knew he had to mentally triage the people on site and sort out the injured in order of the seriousness of their wounds. There would be three scales – the dead (needing no attention), lightly injured (could be driven in a car) and the seriously injured (requiring ambulance). As he weighed this up with the victims around him, the first ambulance arrived, followed very soon by more and some of the fire service vehicles.

By the side of the station there was a man with multiple injuries and he was being looked after by farmers. Francis told the ambulance where to go so that they could get to the same level by driving 50yd down the road, rather than needing the man to be dragged up to the ambulance on the ledge.

Abbeystead may have felt remote, but it wasn't that far from civilisation, being only nine minutes from the motorway, fifteen minutes from the main hospital in Lancaster and twenty-five minutes from a larger hospital at Preston. It was to these two hospitals that the ambulances were now heading with the occupants of the two cars and the people who needed urgent attention.

When he was satisfied that all the support services were on site and his help was no longer required, Francis headed home and back to his children. When he got back, he thanked the next-door neighbours' teenagers, put his two children to bed and settled down to watch the ten o'clock news. The Abbeystead explosion had already made the news and was the big story of the night. He watched someone reply to a query about whether it could have caused by methane: 'No, no it couldn't possibly be.'

When Francis got settled back home, the phone rang. It was a journalist, who had already got his phone number as the local doctor and was calling from a newspaper in Liverpool. He introduced himself and asked, 'Has there been an explosion in Abbeystead?'

'Yes.'

The reporter then asked something bizarre. 'Is everybody there panic stricken?'

'No,' said Francis. 'Everybody is calm, the emergency services are doing everything to the best of their ability and there is no panic.'

The reporter immediately ended the call – it appeared as if he was hoping for a more sensational story. The press were on scene but long after the victims had been taken away. By the time they got there, the incident was over.

Francis did not recognise anyone at the pumping station as being local. All those he saw were strangers, although one of the more seriously injured was the senior official of the water authority and the husband of a woman who had raised a lot of money for a new cancer scanner. This was the man Francis had seen on a lower level and he had told the ambulance to go to him. Although Francis did not know him personally, he was well known in the area. As this was in the days before mobile phones, Francis's wife knew nothing about the explosion until she finally got home from her evening playing tennis.

Meanwhile, over at the hospitals, the first victims had started to arrive. At the Royal Preston Hospital, Gill Ellison was on duty as the senior nurse of the night shift. The shift changeover had been at 20:00 and almost immediately they had taken a call from Ambulance HQ to say there had been an incident at the Abbeystead pumping station and they should expect multiple casualties:

> The major incident plan was implemented and as the call came at changeover of day and night nursing staff ... we had the numbers. We were also the burns unit for the area, which as it turned out was the sort of injuries that the group of visitors suffered from ... extensively. The other remarkable coincidence was ... the local Rotary Club were on a tour of Police HQ [nearby]... some of whose members were in fact consultants at the Royal Preston! It was a very long night.

What surprised her was the amount of empty beds. With few people really that injured, and those that were split between different hospitals, there turned out to be more clergy showing up than victims! With so much trauma going on that night, I asked Gill how she coped with it all mentally and if it had left her traumatised:

> It's not difficult really as we are used to [being] trained to deal with issues like this and work in a team … it's a fine balance between baring your soul and just getting on with it, as that is what we do. I always felt that the Abbeystead folk dealt with it as a community and that outside intervention was not for them.

The final toll was sixteen dead and twenty-eight injured. Twelve of the dead were the visitors, while the other four were NWWA employees. Twenty-four of the injured were visitors, four from the water authority.

Despite the passage of time since the explosion, those who were involved or lived nearby will never forget it. Francis O'Neill remembers the incident like it was yesterday: 'It was the nearest I have ever been to a military medical scenario. Like being in a battlefield. So many injured, so many dead.' Looking back now, he believes that, even if he had his doctor's bag with him, there is very little he could have done owing to the scale of the disaster.

Angela Rothwell lived in the house nearest to the explosion and was shocked when the violent blast rocked her house. She had immediately raised the alarm. Angela remembers the night vividly more than thirty-five years later: 'The police took over our kitchen to provide refreshments for the emergency crews until they got a field kitchen up and running. The press used our telephone all night. My husband was on the news giving an account of what had happened. I have moved now and my husband died six years ago but the memories are still vivid. Such a terrible night.'

Matthew Scott remembers the shock of hearing about the explosion: 'The disaster had a great impact on my family and myself at the time. It was a hot day and myself and my family were in the garden enjoying the weather when we heard about it.'

It was brought closer to home when Matthew heard that two of the victims lived close by:

> I was 12 years old at the time and living in Garstang, which is just 20 miles from Abbeystead. One of the staff from the water works, Jack Lacey, lived on our street; unfortunately he lost his life in the disaster. Also, a young boy who went to my school. I don't remember his name. We just called him by his nickname. He was at my school but not in my classes. I remember he was a well-liked boy but was not really a friend of mine. I do remember him being very clever and in the top sets at school. His dad was something to do with the water board. No one else was injured from my school but Garstang was a very small place and everyone knew someone who knew one or more of the dead. It was quite sombre feeling for a few weeks after.

The young victim Matthew refers to is 12-year-old Mark Eckersley, who died along with his mother Pauline. His father, Thomas, was seriously injured.

Jean Grubb's parents lived and farmed at Caw House, about a mile and a half away from the plant. They had been out at a friend's for the evening and knew nothing about the disaster until Jean made contact at 23:30 that night. She had got her information from her housemates earlier that evening but she thought they must have been mistaken: 'I recall saying there is nothing in Abbeystead for a disaster to happen. How wrong was I?'

That night her parents tried to return back home and were stopped by the police, as the emergency services were still on the scene. Thankfully their route home was open still and they were allowed to proceed on their way. The explosion started several months of hardship for Jean's parents:

> Their water supply [natural spring] was stemmed. They had no water for the home or the animals. Water was delivered by tanker. Four holding tanks were installed in the fields on higher ground to the north of the farmhouse. This continued for months and during the winter the tanks froze. NWW placed straw around the tanks but this was not effective so they added gas heaters, which ultimately exploded and resulted in a fire and emergency evacuation of the animals in the building near the tanks. Logistically this whole episode was a nightmare as Mum and Dad had to carry buckets of water frequently to the animals for quite a prolonged period until a pipeline was eventually provided.

Not only that, Jean's mother then suffered with shingles attributed to the stress of everything that had gone on. This just shows how the knock-on effect can continue for a greater period even when the emergency teams and press have long gone.

The farmers who helped at the scene were mentally scarred for a long time, as were many others who were involved. An investigation into what happened started straight away and a full survey was carried out of the immediate area, which included a seismic scan of the rocks below. By March 1986 it was revealed that a network of geological faults from a gas reservoir had led to methane being leaked into the water system and that, in turn, had led to it being introduced to the valve house, where some kind of spark had ignited the gas.

The legal wrangling between twenty-nine affected parties and the three companies said to be at fault went on for several more years, and as the months passed by the victims' families and those injured seemed to encounter a multitude of hurdles. The legal bills were running into seven-figure sums and, if the people caught up in the tragedy had lost the case, they would have had to sell everything they owned to pay them, including their houses. A local fund set up for the victims raised £80,000. This had been instigated by the *Lancashire Evening Telegraph*, which successfully campaigned to raise money for a relief fund, but this was nothing compared to what was owed to them from the companies and their bills were only going to go up. Out of all the people seeking compensation, only one person was entitled to legal aid, and the rest would have to risk their homes, savings and everything they owned in the hope that justice would be served. All this was stress on top of the injuries and the feelings of loss, which did not seem to fade.

Finally, on 13 March 1987, a High Court judge ruled that the blame for the disaster was split three ways – 55 per cent with Binnie and Partners (the consulting engineers who designed the Abbeystead Water Transfer Scheme), 30 per cent with North West Water Authority, and 15 per cent with builders Edmund Nuttall Ltd. At that point the survivors and relatives of those killed could have got compensation, but Binnie and Partners lodged an appeal and the case dragged on even longer. Eventually it all came to an end in February 1989 when Binnie and Partners reached an out-of-court settlement with the victims thought to be worth over £2 million. The entire process raised the issue of how disaster victims can be put through so much hardship after losing loved ones or being injured. Calls were made to change the law so that people who had suffered as a result of such events should not have to risk everything they owned in order to fight for justice.

The land where the disaster happened is owned by the Duke of Westminster, who uses this area as a grouse- and pheasant-shooting estate. When the inspection chamber was rebuilt and the site brought back to work again, he arranged for a plaque to be positioned there. Even to this day, no serious amount of water goes through this tunnel but a little is allowed through to prevent a build-up of methane. This hopefully ensures that a disaster like that of 1984 will not happen again in this area.

20

1985: Dover Hovercraft Crash

Statistically, hovercraft are one of the safest modes of transport in the world. There have been very few accidents, but that does not mean that there have been none. In 1972 an SR.N6 craft was heading from the Isle of Wight to Southsea (Portsmouth) when it capsized in bad weather, killing five passengers. The disaster was shocking because this type of craft was almost impossible to sink, but a freak turn of events proved that anything is possible.

The much larger SR.N4 was a car- and passenger-carrying ferry hovercraft that in some models could take more than 400 passengers. Six of these were built and the prototype was *The Princess Margaret*.

She was built in 1968 and was originally 130ft long, but lengthened to 185ft later in her career. Powered by four gas turbines, the craft could safely transit across the English Channel at around 40 to 60 knots, meaning a typical Dover–Calais journey would take just half an hour. The owners, Hoverspeed, could cut a regular ferry crossing from hours to just minutes, and you could still take your car using the forward ramp, which led to a spacious car deck. There was enough room for thirty cars initially but that was soon doubled during conversion.

The Princess Margaret was no stranger to incidents in her long career. She suffered wave damage to her bow on 23 September 1968, which put her out of service until 2 October, but incredibly she was damaged again during a crossing just twenty-four hours after going back into service. More wave damage was suffered on 11 October 1980 and just a few months later, on 23 January 1981, she collided with a pier and suffered further hull damage. Thankfully, there were no casualties in any of these incidents but, like the capsized SR.N6, it did show that sometimes hovercraft could be vulnerable when manoeuvring, especially in bad conditions.

John Kobam was a customs officer at the Dover Hoverport at the time and he remembers the difficulties that faced the pilots of these huge craft:

> The seakeeping of the SR.N4 was remarkable but as a dinghy sailor I was well aware that the Western Entrance to Dover Harbour had some of the most challenging conditions in the whole of the Channel. The shape of the walls and the entrance itself meant that there were sometimes strong crosswinds inside the harbour funnelled by the Admiralty pier.

It was Saturday, 30 March 1985, and *The Princess Margaret* was heading towards Dover on her usual run from Calais in a strong wind, under the command of 53-year-old pilot Ian Dalziel, a man with more than fifteen years of experience piloting hovercraft. On board were 370 passengers and eighteen crew. The usual protocol dictated that the craft had to slow down to a reasonable speed in order to enter the harbour, which it did as it approached.

Just outside the harbour was a small tug called the *Dextrous*, which had just finished a job and was heading back in to go alongside. On board was Able Seaman Geoff Delivett, 37, who had started his twenty-four-hour shift that morning at 08:00. The crew consisted of Captain Steve Parsons, Mate Don Terry, Engineer Jim

The Princess Margaret at the Hovercraft Museum in Lee-on-Solent, where she was on display before being scrapped. In 1985 she collided with Dover harbour wall, killing four passengers. (Author)

Very, Able Seaman Dave King and Geoff, who had been on the tugs since July 1979, assisting with the various ships that came and went out of the port and into one of the busiest shipping lanes in the world.

At just after 16:00 they noticed *The Princess Margaret* heading towards the breakwater and about to go into the harbour, but for some reason the craft seemed to be attracted to the 'knuckle' instead of passing in between the two walls. Don remarked with shock, 'That's f★★king close!' with the hovercraft itself obscuring what was happening on the other side.

On board the hovercraft, the crew were struggling to manoeuvre the vessel as the wind was pushing her towards the breakwater, first trying to turn her to port in order to swing the craft into the entrance, then to starboard to pull her around. All this was to no avail, as seconds later the side of the craft crunched into the solid mass of stone which ripped the hull open, creating a huge gash in the passenger area on her starboard side aft. People were flung into the sea and jagged metal stuck out at all angles.

Watching from nearby was the *Dextrous* crew, who were radioed by port control that the hovercraft had collided with the remote knuckle. By now they were off Admiralty Pier No. 3, so they went at full speed towards the site of the disaster. By now the hovercraft was limping into the bay just east of the Prince of Wales Pier. The *Dextrous's* crew were shocked at what they were seeing and went into immediate rescue mode. At the time there was no word on casualties and they saw no signs of people in the water, just a lot of wreckage floating around being swept away by the wind and tides. On board *The Princess Margaret* the crew were frantically trying to help those in need of medical attention, while at the same time trying to rescue the people who had gone overboard. There were over a dozen swimming around in the water injured, the entire side of the craft had been opened up with metal chunks hanging down, the seating areas were now exposed to the elements, and were people trying to move back into the craft and away from danger.

One of the quick-thinking crew members launched a life raft in the hope that those lost overboard could get on board it, but it was heading towards the jagged metal and so he lowered himself into the water to help those people get in; that way he knew that they would be OK. The wind was still very strong and the life raft flipped over, making the officer's job difficult, but he did what he could with what he had.

The *Dextrous* proceeded to close on the survivors, who they could now see. The life raft was drifting and they slowly got close enough to it to throw a heaving line for the people on the raft to grab. However, despite all the instructions shouted to them, there was no reaction; the shock and cold had numbed them into statues. Geoff remembers what happened next:

Without further thought, I jumped into the life raft, lots of water contaminated with fuel inside, and the cold was quite a shock. Inside were a number of French teenagers – I believe they were students – can't remember how many exactly, possibly six, plus an AB from the hovercraft crew. He'd done his bit getting them into the life raft but was then suffering from the cold and shock himself. We then got them aboard the tug, me pushing from below, Jim Very and Dave King hauling from above. By now there were other vessels on-scene, Dover Lifeboat, Harbour Patrol Launch, and Dover motorboats. We proceeded to the tug haven with our casualties. En route I put them (fully clothed) one at a time in a warm shower, and they were given blankets. At the tug haven we handed them over to the ambulance service and proceeded back to the scene.

Wallowing in the harbour, the crippled hovercraft was in serious trouble and still full of hundreds of people. It was a miracle that more had not gone overboard but there was still a very real chance of further danger the longer they were floating around.

The *Dextrous* was nearby with orders to help deal with the casualties on board *The Princess Margaret*. They still had no definite numbers to work with but they began transferring passengers over – as many as they could possibly get on board – in order to ferry them to the tug haven and land them ashore. Geoff remembers taking off 186 people: 'The tug was pretty crowded. During the transfer I stood between the vessels with one foot on each to ensure the safe movement from vessel to vessel. Luckily it was near on level.'

After the passengers were rescued, they then took on board non-essential hovercraft crew members before helping tow the wrecked craft towards the Hoverport, staying on standby all night until the shift was over. As the injured were taken over to Buckland Hospital in Dover, the craft was brought up on to the landing ramp for the damage to be surveyed properly. The hole in the side was around 50ft long and it looked like a bomb had blown the sides of the craft off. But the worst news was that two people had been found dead and another two were still missing, with thirty-six others injured. Dover lifeboat was searching the area hoping to find the two missing bodies in the stormy weather, which incredibly, after a long search, they did.

Just a month later, on 29 April, *The Princess Margaret's* sister craft *The Princess Anne* was damaged by waves in the Channel, which also put her out of service until repairs could be carried out.

In October 1985 an inquest was held into the four deaths, in which the crew gave evidence about what went on in those moments leading up to the collision and the events that followed. The hovercraft captain, Ian Dalziel, rejected the notion that the accident was his fault and instead told the court that the craft had lost power and the controls had failed to respond during the manoeuvre. This was disputed the day after by the director of the British Hovercraft Corporation.

Geoff Delivett remembers the praise he and the tug crew received for their response to the disaster: 'We as a crew received a signed letter from the Duke of Athol of the RNLI commending our actions, and at the inquest I was commended for my efforts in rescuing passengers. But I still feel the loss of the two more to this day.' He remained with Dover Harbour board until he retired as a skipper.

The Princess Margaret was repaired and continued her service as a cross-Channel hovercraft until 2000. Together with *The Princess Anne*, she went on display at the Hovercraft Museum in Lee-on-Solent near Gosport at the old HMS *Daedalus* site, where visitors could marvel at her size. Unfortunately, the owners wanted to redevelop the site and that meant getting rid of the two craft. Working closely with the museum, they finally transferred ownership of the *Anne* to the museum but the *Margaret* was to be cannibalised for spare parts and was broken up for recycling in 2018.

Today there is only one hovercraft service in Britain, a small craft that runs between Southsea and the Isle of Wight. How long that novelty will last is anybody's guess.

21

1990: Sinking of the *Flag Theofano*

On 29 January 1990, a great storm had blown towards the coast of Hampshire and was causing havoc with the marine traffic coming in and out of the Solent area. For those in charge of the waterways in the busy ports of Southampton and Portsmouth, trying to deal with the ships that needed berths to unload their cargo was a nightmare. As with any major port, there has to be order when it comes to the flow of traffic; a ship coming in would prevent another leaving at the same time, unless they crossed paths in a part of the Channel that was wide enough to accommodate both vessels. Even then there would be the risk of them getting too close to one another, and in bad weather it would never have been worth the added danger. On top of that, there were vessels that had to be guided in by the local harbour pilot, who would meet the ship out at sea in a small motor boat and then take charge of its journey into port.

That evening the Greek cement carrier *Flag Theofano* was one of those ships inbound for Southampton after a short voyage across the Channel from Le Havre with a crew of nineteen on board – eleven Greek, seven Moldavian and one Egyptian. At 2,818 gross tons, the 20-year-old cargo ship was 324ft long, having been

The cargo vessel *Flag Theofano*, which sank in the Solent in January 1990.

built in Germany. She had changed ownership several times, and changed her name more than once as well.

Launched as the *Boston Express*, she then became the *Ino A* (1971–74), *Rabat* (1974–80), *Victoria* (1980–May 1989) and finally the *Flag Theofano*. Under the new ownership of the Golden Union Shipping Company of Piraeus, she was converted to carry bulk cargo of cement and was chartered under a three-year contract by the cement manufacturer Blue Circle to carry their products around the world.

She had arrived in Le Havre five days earlier and cement was poured into her cargo holds via a huge pipe that was fed via a conveyor belt. Waiting alongside for the next few days for the cement to settle, she sailed on 29 January at 11:28 under the local pilot before she headed off under her own commanding officer towards Southampton. This was a journey of only a few hours, but it was obvious when the ship set off that the weather was getting steadily worse.

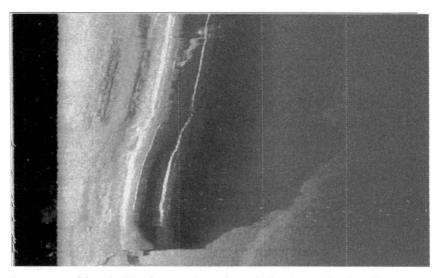

Sonar scan of the *Flag Theofano* wreck on the seabed. (Martin Woodward)

With a dirty grey hull and two large deck cranes towering over her forward and aft hatches and facing each other, her squat yellow funnel gently eased the amount of exhaust smoke that was produced from her engines as she slowed her speed and rounded the eastern tip of the Isle of Wight. At this point she was in the shipping separation lanes that made sure the busy Solent area was kept danger-free, and she promptly made radio contact with Southampton's vessel traffic service, which was in accordance with the usual procedures for entering port.

Due to the sea state being too rough, they were unable to provide the *Flag Theofano* with a pilot that evening, so she was called on the radio and told to go to anchor for the night at an area of the Solent known as St Helens Roads. Agreeing to this change of plan, the crew acknowledged it and headed towards the anchorage.

Forty-four-year-old Captain Ioannis Pittas was then able to drop anchor and relax for the evening, leaving the worry about getting alongside until the next day. Pittas had only taken over command of the *Flag Theofano* a few weeks earlier but already had made this journey enough times to know what was required. The ship made her last radio call at 19:23, during which she gave her position and intentions for anchoring and the preparations made to ride out the bad weather until the morning.

At around 20:00 a passing ship noted her at the anchorage area, and there was nothing to suggest that anything was, or would be, amiss. The winds were at around 60mph and the seas choppy; anybody who sailed in this weather in a small craft would not survive.

At around midnight, the radio operator at Southampton VTS attempted to contact the ship several times but received no reply. This was not unheard of so nobody was particularly worried.

At 01:00 the nearby Bembridge lifeboat was called out and launched to search for an intoxicated man who may have gone swimming in the sea. However, thankfully, the person in question was located still on shore and so the search was called off, with the boat heading back to the station.

As dawn broke the next morning, it brought no better weather, but the berthing arrangements had already been put in place and the *Flag Theofano* was given the green light to weigh anchor and proceed into Southampton, with a pilot vessel heading towards St Helens Road to meet the ship. However, when she was called on the radio there was again no reply. The Southampton pilot vessel made its way out past Calshot Castle and eastbound towards the anchorage, but when it reached St Helens Road at just after 09:00 there was no ship to be seen. The pilot radioed the port authority in confusion.

Vessels in the area were called and a search carried out, but the ship had simply vanished. Had she already gone somewhere else for shelter? The search intensified and that morning the full horror was realised when a lifeboat bearing the ship's name, a life raft and two bodies (those of Captain Pittas and Second Officer Hariton Skaltsaris) were found at the nearby West Wittering Beach by people walking their dog. It was now obvious: the *Flag Theofano* had gone down in the night and not a single person had known about it. There had been no radio calls and no eyewitnesses. Immediately, helicopters were launched and every ship in the area, every lifeboat and whatever aircraft that could be scrambled were now on the lookout for any survivors.

The wreck of the ship was located by 15:30 the same day, when an oily patch on the water along with a stream of bubbles was discovered that marked the spot, along with some unknown object that was still attached to the wreck just below the surface on the end of a rope. Almost 66ft below the surface, the ship with her cargo of 4,000 tons of cement was upside down on the seabed. At their first chance of a break in the weather, divers ventured down to the wreck.

Isle of Wight diver Martin Woodward lived in a house overlooking the area where the ship went down and he was tasked with inspecting the wreck in the days following the sinking. He was not only a diver, but one of the RNLI volunteer crew, and he had been out on the Bembridge lifeboat the night the ship had sunk searching for the assumed-missing swimmer. The Royal Navy had already tried to get down to the wreck the day after the sinking, but the weather had prevented them from completing their mission. The visibility was just too bad and the weather was not showing any signs of letting them safely descend and inspect the ship. They had to wait until it was safe enough, and even then this *was* the Solent. As divers found when working on the wreck of the Tudor warship *Mary Rose* ten years previously, it is never a good place to be able to see clearly.

Martin and his team arrived at the wreck several days later but again nothing could be seen with the naked eye, even when they got down there. A buoy was attached to the wreck, and after feeling around the huge hulk, the rest of the investigation was carried out by sonar sweeps from the surface in order to learn as much as possible from the position of the ship and how she lay on the seabed. There were no noises coming from the upturned hull that would indicate survivors trapped on board, but the team still offered to cut a hole in the ship to release the bodies of the missing crew. Unfortunately, by now nobody was interested in taking responsibility for hiring a team to get the rest of the crew out and where they were left inside the sunken wreck, where they still remain today.

Over time, the bodies of just five of the crew were discovered, including the two that were found on the beach within hours of the sinking. The rest of them had the *Flag Theofano* as their permanent tomb. By now the ship's cargo had come into contact with the sea water and hardened, leaving the wreck nothing more than a huge concrete block surrounded by the hull of the ship. There was never any sign of the fourteen missing crew members and the cause of her loss was initially thought to be capsizing due to bad weather possibly shifting the cargo. Another theory was that the Dean Tail Buoy, which had been damaged in a previous storm, may have been in the way and, unlit, it was quite feasible that the ship could have turned sharply to avoid this marker. A sharp sudden turn would have shifted the cargo and caused a disaster so quickly that there would have been no time to even pick up the radio and call for help. However, an investigation was under way, albeit progressing slowly, and all possibilities would have to be explored one at a time.

In the aftermath of the disaster, the Greek shipping owner simply blamed the port authorities for not allowing the vessel safe passage alongside, completely forgetting that it was too dangerous for a pilot launch to come out and guide the vessel in. Blue Circle denied that the ship was on a time limit and said that their stocks of cement were high enough to not have to risk lives to get a ship to a port in such a dangerous condition and put the pilot in danger.

On 1 July 1991 the inquest into the deaths of the nineteen crew was opened in the town of Chichester by West Sussex coroner Mark Calvert-Lee. The first witness to be called was port agent Roger Thornton of Wainwright Brothers, who would have been responsible for the ship when she got into Southampton. On day two, diver Martin Woodward put a lot of rumours to rest regarding the causes of the sinking, which included the theory that a rope had been caught around the propellers. One by one the witnesses and experts gave their version of events, and after three days of hearing the evidence from more than twenty witnesses, the jury delivered a verdict of misadventure on the deaths of all nineteen crew.

On 14 July, the Marine Accident Investigation Branch published their official report into the sinking. After more than a year of researching and detective work, a shift in her cargo of cement was blamed as the sole cause of the disaster.

As for *Flag Theofano* herself, plans were put forward to remove the wreck and there was even talk of blowing her up due to her remains being a navigational hazard, but with the huge costs involved none of these ideas were carried out and the *Flag Theofano* today lies where she sank, her position clearly marked on the charts and also by marker buoys.

The loss of this vessel and her crew of nineteen is a f modern-day disaster that is barely remembered by anybody who was not directly involved in it. There are no memorials to the victims and one of the five bodies found is buried in Portsmouth's Kingston Cemetery with no gravestone to mark the man's passing. Able Seaman Ibrahim Hussain was from the Maldives and just 19 years old when he became a victim of this shipwreck that is today barely talked about. The other four bodies were sent back to their native Greece for burial.

22

1993: Southampton Airport Crash

In January 1989 a Boeing 737 crashed on to the M1 motorway in Leicester, killing forty-seven people and leaving dozens more injured. Incredibly, none of the traffic passing by at the time was hit by the aircraft. On several occasions throughout the world there have been disasters where air crashes on main roads have led to several deaths and major injuries, but on the M27 motorway near Southampton in 1993 there was an accident that had surprisingly positive results.

On 26 May 1993, an aircraft was awaiting permission to land at Southampton (Eastleigh) Airport after a short flight from Oxford. The 12-year-old Cessna 550 Citation II executive jet had seating for nine people but on this day carried no passengers, just the pilot and co-pilot making the regular scheduled commute between the two airports. Following a rainy night, the runway was wet and carried a large amount of water. Eight passengers were due to board the aircraft for a short flight to Eindhoven and the airport was preparing for an early arrival, which would be around half an hour before the airport officially opened at 06:00.

A heavy thunderstorm was making visibility difficult, but they were given clearance to land and the wheels touched down on the runway. With a heavy tail wind and very wet runway to contend with, the aircraft suddenly went out of control and could not be brought to a stop. The end of the runway was getting closer and the pilots tried frantically to reduce speed, but nothing could be done.

The Cessna smashed through the airport barrier fence, plunged down an embankment and on to the M27, spinning 180 degrees and finally coming to a stop in the central barrier, crashing into two vehicles along the way. The aircraft began leaking fuel on to the motorway and, to the horror of those who could see it, the plane then burst into flames.

Quickly shutting down the engines, the pilot and co-pilot opened an emergency exit and swiftly exited the Cessna. The three occupants of the two cars managed to get out and away from the burning aircraft, and incredibly none of their injuries were serious.

Adrian Walder was a traffic patrol officer assigned to the motor-cycle unit on this day. He preferred to use a normal police car but today he was on the bike again, which was handy for weaving in and out of traffic to reach the scene of accidents. It had taken him a long time to get this job; officers had to wait their turn to be chosen, and since he had joined the police eighteen years earlier he had worked in many different roles, such as escorting category A prisoners and being a firearms officer.

This morning, Adrian got up at around 06:30 and put the kettle on. Today he was assigned to the day shift, which started at 08:00 and finished at 16:00, his responsibility being to patrol the A27 but not the motorway nearby. As he was making his first cup of tea of the day he put the TV on to catch the news and saw the first reports of a plane crash on the M27.

Stunned by the thought of a major incident on his patch, he picked up the police radio that he was allowed to take home every night and called up the control room. They told him to go straight to the scene of the crash and so he raced to get his uniform on and left the house. His bike was under his car port and within minutes

Eyewitness photograph of the M27 motorway plane crash, 1993. (Courtesy Martin Cole)

he was speeding away from his home north-west of his station at Eastleigh and out towards the M27.

It was not long before he realised just how much chaos the crash was causing. The traffic was at a standstill everywhere, and the fact it was rush hour made it even worse. Thankfully, his motorcycle could get to the scene a lot quicker than the cars and he headed towards the motorway at Junction 5 after taking a number of back roads to beat the gridlock.

Just before he got to the junction, he ended up near the fire station at Eastleigh and was just in time to see one of the fire engines heading out using its blue lights and sirens. Unfortunately, a nearby lorry was not paying attention and the fire truck drove straight into it right in front of him. Adrian stopped to make sure that everybody was OK, the drivers exchanging details before they could move again. The fire chief had no time to lose and so he hitched a ride on the back of Adrian's bike; they were soon speeding off, the fireman using his firefighting helmet as a motorbike helmet. The fire officer was actually on his way to a different incident, so Adrian had to drop him off before continuing his original task.

By the time Adrian reached the burnt-out aircraft the major part of the incident had already been taken care of. He talked to the incident commander at the scene and saw that diversions were already in place and that traffic was slowly being moved.

His priority was the welfare of his team. He had all the kit at the scene, but he needed updates on the people involved in the rescue and cordoning operations. For the next hour and half, he went around the diversions checking up on other officers to make sure they were OK. They were usually with vehicles and the officers had to stay with them, parking across roads with hard barriers and cones with them. Colleagues were dropped off at other points and relieved those who had been stood there for hours. He went to the nearest shop and asked the people who ran it if his officers could use their facilities.

The next task was to call out the official police photographer and the Air Accidents Investigation Branch, who turned up that afternoon to start their investigations escorted by Adrian's colleagues. Looking over at the aircraft from a distance, it was amazing how so few people had been injured – let alone killed – in this crash.

The traffic did not ease up until later on that day, but in the congestion the control room deployed Adrian to Rownams to meet a donor car that was rushing a heart to Southampton General Hospital. Adrian escorted the car as fast as possible and successfully got the organ to the hospital in good time. The driver of the car said it was the most exciting trip he had ever had!

As the stories of the crash were being told between officers, everybody was relieved that only minor medical attention was required. Adrian's 'whirlwind of a day' ended at around 15:00, when he finally stopped for a bite to eat. It was now up to the recovery teams, who spent the rest of the operation removing the wreckage and reopening the M27 lanes.

The following few days saw incredible stories appear in the press afterthe occupants of the cars were interviewed. It soon became apparent just how close to death they had all been, when one car was recovered from almost under the aircraft and another had been turned over on to its roof. Both had suffered significant damage.

The official Air Accidents Investigation Branch report a year later found the pilot to blame, as he had attempted to land in a tail wind that was outside of safe limits.

23

1995: Knight Air Flight 816 Crash

Air disasters are not common within the United Kingdom and most inquiries carried out by the Air Accidents Investigation Branch involve light aircraft. However, there are times when a more major incident occurs and answers need to be found quickly, especially when they involve passengers on commercial flights. On Wednesday, 24 May 1995, nobody expected a quiet country farm would be the scene of such a horrific incident such as this, especially when just twenty-four hours earlier Britain had been shocked by another disaster, a coach crash on the M4 that killed thirteen people on a Royal British Legion day out. That day's newspapers were both shocking and sad to read, but something equally tragic was to happen that would quickly replace the crash on the front pages.

An air disaster emergency plan had not been set up for the area around North Yorkshire in the mid 1990s as the local authorities were convinced that nothing untoward would happen on their patch, as the nearest airport was Teesside and the chances of a crash were very remote. However, this was not true, as whoever was in charge had neglected to consisder Leeds Bradford, a very busy regional airport that had opened in 1931 as Leeds and Bradford

Municipal Aerodrome and grown larger over the years. By now there were several major airlines running commuter flights from there going up and down the country, using aircraft up to the size of small passenger jets.

One of the regional airlines that operated from Leeds Bradford was Knight Air, which had been purchased in 1992 by the Lambson Group of Harrogate for £1.2 million. Based at Leeds Bradford, they ran a fleet of six aircraft – four Embraer Bandeirantes and two Cessna light business aircraft. The airline was officially launched in 1988 under the name Knightway Air Charter, operating a helicopter air taxi service. The aim was to be Yorkshire's only regional airline in the charter and scheduled flights market. It was only in January 1994 that Knight Air started running twice-daily scheduled flights to Aberdeen. As well as this they also ran flights to Belfast, Southampton, Teesside and the Isle of Man.

Knight Air expanded immediately by first taking over Budge Aviation, part of the collapsed BF Budge empire, and then taking over from Yorkshire European when it went into liquidation in November 1993. That gave it two twin-engined turboprop Embraer Bandeirante 110P commuter aircraft, made in Brazil, one of which was G-OEAA. A third was added to the fleet when it began operating flights from Leeds to Belfast in October 1994 following the Ulster ceasefire. Knight Air was one of several 'type B' airlines in Britain licensed to fly aircraft of between two and nineteen seats. By 1995 the airline had ninety staff.

The Bandeirante was a reliable aircraft. With twenty-one seats in total for both the passengers and two pilots, they were just under 50ft long with a top speed of 286mph. The aircraft had made its maiden flight in 1968, with production beginning four years later, and it had since been sold around the world. The engines were Canadian-built Pratt and Whitneys.

G-OEAA had been delivered brand new to Jersey European Airways in 1980 and had been used by several companies before

An aerial photograph of the crash scene released by North Yorkshire Police.
(Courtesy North Yorkshire Police)

being taken over by Knight Air in 1993. The plane was below the
weight limit to have a compulsory black box fitted, therefore it did
not have one; neither did it have weather radar.

Knight Air had a good reputation. The passengers were given a
choice of where to sit when they boarded and the crew were known
to be friendly. Although the plane was very basic, the airline did
give passengers coffee and biscuits on the short journey. The pilot,
who did not have a separate cabin, would make his announcements
simply by turning around and talking to the passengers behind him.

Knight Air flight 816 was now on the tarmac at Leeds Bradford
Airport ready to depart with just nine passengers and three crew.
The crew consisted of 49-year-old pilot John Casson, co-pilot Paul
Denton, 38, and stewardess Helen Leadbetter, 22. Helen had only
worked for Knight Air for three months after quitting her previous
job as a dental nurse. Her boyfriend was 27-year-old insurance
broker Tim Marshall.

Paul had achieved his ambition of becoming an airline pilot just
five weeks previously, after dreaming about it since he was a child.

The aircraft that crashed on 24 May 1995 killing all twelve people on board in the village of Dunkeswick. (Courtesy Jon Wornham)

Working hard through his life to get where he wanted, he married his wife, Tracey, only two weeks previously. He started by accompanying his father, Tony, on jaunts in small planes when he was a young boy. Once Paul had left school he got a job as a builder to pay for flying lessons, qualifying as a private pilot in 1991, and finally becoming an airline pilot four years later. He lived in Highburton, near Huddersfield.

John Casson had 3,257 hours' flying experience and had previously been in a 1993 advert for Yorkshire European Airlines, appearing in a photograph as a first officer with other pilots and aircrew. Next to this photograph was the Bandeirante G-BTAA, which was later re-registered G-OEAA – the one he would be taking to Aberdeen today.

Although the company had a good safety record, a Knight Air Bandeirante had suffered an engine problem and been forced to make an emergency landing at RAF Leeming on 9 May, although no one was hurt.

The passengers were now boarded and ready. One of these was Irene Wolsey, who was heading to visit her son, daughter-in-law and grandchildren in St Cyrus. Another was 61-year-old Bill Ingram, who was a contracts manager with Morrison Construction and was involved in projects such as St Fergus gas terminal.

The weather forecast was looking dismal. There had been sunshine and clear skies but this changed at around 16:00 when the weather took a turn for the worst with torrential rain and a thunderstorm lasting for around twenty minutes, then again half an hour later. Dark clouds gathered and visibility became a major issue, with it going down to around 2.5 miles and just 1,600ft by 18:00.

As the weather worsened, Knight Air flight 816 sped down the runway and took off at 17:46, due to land in Aberdeen around 18:35.

But just three minutes into the flight, air traffic controller Malcolm Bedford received a message from Knight Air 816 requesting permission to return to the airport. When Malcolm asked what the problem was, they radioed back that there seemed to be an issue with the aircraft's artificial horizon. The weather by now was very poor with rain, low cloud and thunderstorms.

The radar screens showed the plane as it climbed to 3,600ft, turning continuously left apart from an abrupt right turn while passing 1,700ft. Despite these turns, the crew sought confirmation that the aircraft was still 'going straight' and shortly after reaching 3,600ft the plane entered a steeply descending spiral dive and then disappeared from the screen.

★★★

One and a half miles away from the A61 Harrogate to Leeds road in North Yorkshire lies the tiny village of Dunkeswick. It is in an area few people had heard of, consisting of farmers' fields, a few houses and the village of Weeton at the end of a narrow road.

Nearby, Neil Duffy was filling his GS850 Suzuki motorbike with fuel at a petrol station after a long day at work. As he finished, he suddenly heard a large bang followed by a smaller one. He looked around but could not see a thing; the rain was so heavy it was impossible to make out where it had come from. He thought no more about it and headed home.

Local farmer David Rayner was outside working on his land when he heard the noise of an aircraft, seemingly very low with what sounded like a 'bad noise' coming from the engines. A sudden bang was then met by absolute silence. The shock of what David heard had him racing indoors to call his neighbouring farmer, Michael Webster.

Michael lived on Main Street in Weeton and was in his house having a cup of tea when David called to say what he had heard. He assumed that a plane had crashed into his field and suggested that Michael go check it out in case people needed help. Michael raced off with his 15-year-old daughter to have a look, the poor visibility across the fields not making it easy. From what he saw, his field was clear, so perhaps the noise David heard was further away.

In the meantime, David had jumped into his Land Rover and headed out to see what he could find elsewhere.

A few miles away was the stately home and museum of Harewood House, where bird garden curator John Waller had been managing the site for around fifteen years. There had been an event that day and he was clearing up after everybody had gone home, which would mean him working late into the evening. He noticed how foggy it had got as the evening went on. 'You couldn't see ten feet in front of you!' he recalled. Talking to his boss, they both stopped when they heard the noise of an aircraft flying nearby. It sounded like it was coming from the direction of the airport and they found it strange that it should be flying in conditions like this. The noise of the engine had his boss remark, 'that sounds like it's in trouble', as they looked to the sky. The engines were screaming, it seemed, but they saw nothing in the fog. Suddenly a bang got their attention, followed by silence.

A number of people heard the aircraft and the resulting bang, but one man saw more than the rest. Forty-year-old Keith Elliott lived in the first house in Weeton and was at home this day as he never usually worked on a Wednesday. He had been out for lunch earlier in the day and now he was surveying some building work outside. He did not find the rain too bad, so he had left his coat and just had his shirt on. It was only drizzle, he thought.

All of a sudden he heard a sound, 'what sounded like oooooowwwwwww, followed by a boom', as he turned to see the aircraft in the air just before the sound came of it crashing into the nearby field. He jumped into his wife's Range Rover and drove as fast as he could to the top of the hill. Shocked at what he saw, he dialled 999 with the car phone and told the operator what he had just witnessed before he got out and walked towards the site.

When he got there he was greeted by a field littered with flames, wreckage and bodies. He rang 999 again to report further details and that there were multiple fatalities. When he started counting the bodies he then realised that this was not just a light aircraft. He thought, 'How big was this plane?' as he headed back to the car again. He quickly rang his wife to tell her to keep his dinner in the oven, as there had been a plane crash. He turned the car around and blocked off the road in Weeton to stop anybody but the emergency services from entering. By now people were curious and turning up to see what had happened, but he prevented them from going past.

Over at Harewood House, John Waller started hearing sirens and was confused as to why fire engines were making their way towards the building. When they realised that they had taken a wrong turning, the fire engines turned around and exited the grounds, knocking over barriers in the process. Several reports were going out by now that there had been a plane crash in the grounds of Harewood House, or close to it.

The first 999 calls had been received at 17:58 by North Yorkshire Fire and Rescue reporting the crash of a light aircraft 6 miles north-east of the airport at Dunkeswick. The first emergency services arrived on scene at 18:12, twenty-two minutes after the aircraft had been lost from radar.

It was now obvious that Knight Air flight 816 had crashed in a 45-acre barley field owned by the Trickett family, the crops being at around thigh height. The small road was now full of ambulances, fire engines and police cars, as well as onlookers and locals. The area had to be sealed off and by the evening around 200 members of the emergency services were on scene.

A Sea King helicopter arrived from RAF Leconfield and hovered over the site, whereupon the wreckage was seen to be spread for hundreds of yards across the field, cutting a 100-yd swathe across the barley.

Keith Elliott was still at the cordon he had made to prevent traffic coming through. His trousers were a mess from his trudging through the field. He looked over at the helicopter and saw that the police had now blocked off the road all the way from the A61 right up to where he had blocked it from the Weeton side. It was dark by now and he had been there for several hours. The press had started to arrive and began talking to him about what he had seen, but when the police took over his job with their own car, he was free to drive away and go home.

Paul Kernaghan, Assistant Chief Constable of North Yorkshire Police, was put in charge of the incident:

I think I had just got home – I was living on my own at the time, having recently transferred to North Yorkshire and my wife and daughter were back in the West Midlands visiting – and was trying to make a meal, when the DCC, John Giffard, telephoned to tell me about the crash and that the incident was mine as ACC Operations. My first thoughts were that this was a real introduction to my role.

I think I arrived at the scene less than an hour after that first call and realised that we were not dealing with a rescue scenario but rather with a recovery and investigation situation. I was also very conscious that, despite being in a remote part of North Yorkshire, we already had satellite news teams there.

The site was now completely secured, roads were blocked off, the teams were in place and everybody was where they should be. This was the first air disaster that this area had had to deal with for twenty-one years. In December 1974, eight people had been killed after their plane had taken off from Leeds Bradford Airport and crashed soon after, with the pilot thought to have had a heart attack.

Flames could be seen dotted around the field but these small fires were quickly extinguished as soon as the fire brigade arrived. Pamphlets were littering the area showing passengers what to do in an emergency on board the flight. It was obvious now that there were no survivors, and at 19:04 the request was put out for body bags to be brought to the scene and the coroner was on his way. That evening all twelve victims were accounted for and had been declared dead by a doctor. North Yorkshire and Greater Manchester Police joined members of Swaledale Fell Rescue to comb the crash site, marking all pieces of wreckage and property with poles placed into the ground.

Anthony Hunt was returning to his home in Dunkeswick after working at his office in Harrogate that evening. It had been a dreadful day for weather – very overcast – and he had decided to come home early. But when he got to the bottom of Weeton Lane he saw that something was not right by the amount of traffic around. It was never this busy, so there had to be an incident of some kind. Local Tony Piccard came out and saw him, telling him that there had been a plane crash nearby. He managed to get home and saw his wife Enid, who said that she had heard a terrible explosion but had not seen anything in the fog and rain.

When he found out as much as he could, he went to offer his services to the emergency teams. Not all their vehicles could get into the field, but his Land Rover could and he helped them load their specialist equipment into his car and take it over for them. He did not venture as far into the field as to see any bodies, but he did see wreckage sticking out of the barley. Once he had done that he went back home to help his wife make tea for the emergency services, who were working long into the night. A Women's Royal Voluntary Services canteen arrived from Otley and Harrogate later to provide meals and refreshments for the dozens of work-ers examining the wreckage. They were there from the morning after the crash and stayed on site for eight days. They ran their base from an army tent, preparing and cooking meals at a high school in Harrogate and bringing it on site. They thought they would only be there for four days, but it was soon realised that this would need to be extended and volunteers had to be arranged to cover the extra days.

The press were gathering as much information as they could but the police did not want them getting too close. Instead they interviewed the locals, among them Tony and Enid.

The roads remained blocked off for the next few days. The first responders had long gone, the fire teams had completed their jobs and the twelve bodies had been photographed in situ before being taken by army ambulances and escorted by the police to RAF Linton-on-Ouse near York.

Counselling was offered to those who were first on the scene and lived nearby, along with the emergency crews who had to trek through the field and deal with the bodies, but many of them refused it. The wreckage of the aircraft was moved on to trucks by soldiers of 2nd Signals Regiment based at Imphal Barracks in York.

★★★

The morning after the crash, Thursday, 25 May, shortly before 10:00, the police were joined by representatives of the Civil Aviation Authority and the Air Accidents Investigation Branch. Knight Air had not suspended any of their flights pending an investigation but had offered to take relatives to the crash site, although they would not confirm to the press how many had accepted this offer. As well as the AAIB, a team was flying out from Rio to help investigators as the plane was a Brazilian-built aircraft and they would need expert opinion from the manufacturers.

One thing that was touched upon a lot in the day's newspaper headlines, as well as in TV reports, was the story of a young boy who may have heard something. In Kendal in Cumbria, Steven Saunders switched his radio scanner on that evening to listen to the aircraft traffic and overheard a conversation between an aircraft and the control tower. He heard an aircraft report that they had been hit by lightning and had an engine problem, then the radio went fuzzy before going off. It was later that night that his father heard about the crash and linked the two events. Was this Knight Air 816 in the last seconds of her flight? Steven claimed to have heard the numbers 8 and 6 being called and said the pilot was calm. Was this a hoax? Was he mistaken and had picked up a different flight with issues? Nothing more was reported about this.

Meanwhile, at the closest church to the crash, St Barnabas Church in Weeton, a candle-lit service was held on 27 May that many of the victims' relatives attended. It would be another four days before the last of the wreckage was finally taken away to Farnborough in Hampshire, the headquarters of the AAIB.

In the next few weeks the crash was covered continuously by the local newspapers but not much appeared in the national press. Funerals and inquests were the main theme for now. On 2 June 1995, West Yorkshire coroner David Hinchliff opened the inquest and gave brief details of the crash before it was adjourned.

By now sixteen police officers had been taken off normal duties to help the families of the victims, with at least one officer assigned to each family. They would liaise with the relatives as the inquest and investigation progressed, arranging transport for those who could go. Other tasks included dealing with financial problems and arranging the funerals. Some had been taken to the crash site, shielded from the media, so they could see it for themselves. The identification of bodies was carried out by using items of clothing or personal effects as it was impossible to do it visually.

An interim report by investigators on 7 June stated that the plane broke up before impact and that it had descended from 3,600ft, descending in a spiral. The pilots were flying blind, acknowledging the instructions from air traffic control but still going left instead of right.

The funeral of pilot John Casson was held on the same day in the village of Luddenden, near Halifax, attended by his wife Pam and his children, Thomas and Louise. Two hours later, Helen Leadbetter's funeral took place at St John the Baptist Church in Coley, to which John Casson's widow sent flowers.

One month later, AAIB investigators flew a Knight Air plane of the exact same type close to the crash site in an effort to reconstruct the last moments. It retraced the route the plane followed and allowed investigators to calibrate the radar signature and make sure it matched the correct distance from the ground. Part of the activity involved flying low over the crash site and making several low swoops in order to assess the accuracy of the airfield radar. Police warned villagers not to be alarmed.

So far, Knight Air itself had not been implicated in any wrongdoing, but that did not mean the company did not suffer. They had lost two pilots and a stewardess as well as their aircraft. By 1 March 1996 the airline had ceased to run commercial flights from Leeds Bradford to Aberdeen and that route was allocated to another airline, Manx Airlines Express (operating as a BA franchise). Commercial director Tim Russell said that the decision had not been influenced by the crash, stating that larger Jetstream aircraft were already being planned to cope with increasing traffic and that Lambson would be concentrating more on its engineering operation.

On the first anniversary of the crash, a report in the *Yorkshire Evening Post* said that Tracey Denton, the widow of co-pilot Paul Denton, had not received a single penny from Knight Air. By now the company was just a faded memory.

A memorial service was held at St Barnabas Church in Weeton and it was here that a memorial plaque in Yorkshire stone was unveiled, paid for by locals, the council and companies including the now defunct Knight Air. Costing £3,000, the inscription reads simply: 'Remember before God those who died in the air disaster at Dunkeswick on 24 May 1995. May they rest in the peace of Christ.'

The memorial was officially dedicated by Rt Rev David Young, and later a service was led by the Rector of Kirkby Overblow, Rev. Paul Summers, which was attended by the Mayor and Mayoress of Harrogate. That night twelve candles were lit, one for each victim, at St Barnabas Church, just a mile from the scene of so much devastation twelve months before.

As the investigators finished their work, on 27 June 1996 the official accident report blamed the failure of one or both of the plane's artificial horizon screens, a display that allows the crew to keep the plane level even in bad visibility. The plane had no standby horizon, nor did it need to have one. The pilot was newly promoted and the co-pilot newly qualified, and putting them together should have been avoided as it meant that the crew's ability to handle an emergency would have been impaired. The report recommended that any aircraft with more than nine seats should have a third horizon as well as a 'black box' flight recorder. It also recommended that the CAA should ensure there was an overall standard for artificial horizons and improved maintenance for UK-registered Bandeirantes.

The aircraft had not experienced total electrical failure and apart from the horizons there were no other airworthiness problems. The report said that it should have been possible to use other instruments. However, it was also revealed that the instruments did not have to be checked regularly; instead, they would await a failure and then they would be reported as unserviceable by the flight crew. It will never be known if one or both artificial horizons failed. Repeated failures on similar aircraft had led to Knight Air alone removing eighteen horizons from their Bandeirante fleet for maintenance in the sixteen months prior to the crash, and one had been used for as little as twenty hours' flying. On top of this there were inconsistencies in documentation that led to confusion for the operator.

The aircraft spiralled out of control and was already breaking up and on fire before it hit the ground. 'Due to an airspeed in excess of the design maximum, the aircraft began to break up with the wing failing outboard of the right-hand engine, tail plane failure, disruption of the fuselage and the early stages of a fuel-fed fire,' said the report.

On 18 November 1996 an inquest led by West Yorkshire coroner David Hinchliff was opened in Leeds, first hearing evidence from the official AAIB report. Nineteen witnesses were called to give evidence and pathologist Professor Michael Green stated that the sudden loss of cabin pressure would have ensured that the deaths were quick and those on board would have lost consciousness before the plane hit the ground. He said that the plane went into a spin at a speed exceeding 250 knots, leading to depressurisation of the cabin.

The jury of three women and six men were sworn in, while a tenth juror stood down after he revealed that his niece worked for Knight Air at the time of the crash.

After nine days of evidence, on 28 November 1996, the jury returned a verdict of accidental death after three hours and forty minutes of deliberation. Their conclusion was that the crash was caused by a combination of instrument malfunction, poor weather conditions and spatial disorientation of the pilots. The coroner had directed the jury to consider only an open verdict or one of accidental death, despite a request for one of unlawful killing from the families' solicitor. The verdict was met with silence and sobbing, but the families were now free to take legal action against the companies involved.

On 6 December 1996 the CAA revealed that more than 130 aircraft were operating without the safety improvements recommended after the crash. It was recommended that aircraft should have three horizons, with the third one having its own independent power supply. If one failed this could be used to confirm the readings of the remaining one. In discussion with the manufacturer, it was decided that Bandeirantes would have to have a third horizon in order to obtain a British licence, but ten other types of aircraft were still not conforming to this. At that time there were around 400 Bandeirantes being operated around the world.

On 18 May 1997 it was announced that the families of ten of the victims would be taking six companies to court for compensation, after it was revealed that after months of negotiations there had been no reasonable offer of compensation. Those companies were:

1. Lambson Aviation (trading as Knight Air)
2. Embraer
3. BF Goodrich Avionics Systems
4. Aviation Instrument Manufacturing Corporation
5. Jet Electronics and Technology
6. CSE Aviation

John Casson's widow Pam said she would not be taking part due to the amount of time already taken and her need to move on from the crash. The legal action was set to take between one and two years before reaching a conclusion. Instead, she started legal action against Knight Air herself. This is because the families of the pilot and co-pilot, while being cleared of all blame, had to act separately from those of the passengers and stewardess in case the standard of the pilots' flying was called into question.

The 1929 Warsaw Convention set out a limit of £100,000 compensation on air accident cases and the families were hoping to overturn this.

Their legal action finally came to an end on 5 March 1998, when it was revealed that eight passengers and the stewardess were awarded an out-of-court settlement of £1 million between them. The family of Irene Wolsey were deemed to be financially independent from her and therefore unable to receive compensation. Casson's case was still ongoing at this time. Due to the nature of the settlement, exact details were not disclosed to the public.

Despite this being a headline-hitting disaster, few people who even close to the site today even realise that something had happened there. Those who were there that night will never forget it, and neither will the families of those who died. In the village of Luddenden a long list of villagers who have no nearby burial is etched into the pathway, with the name of John Casson being one of them. The memories of this accident will fade over time and, once again, the names of the villages involved will be consigned to the history books. All that remains is a small memorial stone in a village church that honours those who died on 24 May 1995.

Afterword

So, after a journey across the country researching two dozen disasters, it amazes me just how different – yet still similar – a lot of them are. Each of these disasters had traumatised survivors, and many rescue workers were still seeing the faces of the disasters' victims long after the sites had been cleared up and made safe. These events, dating back almost 200 years, had the same shocking effect on their society as they do today.

In the days before twenty-four-hour news channels dominated the TV screens and social media became the number-one platform on which to share information, you were left with flimsy reports in newspapers the size of tables, with page one dedicated to advertisements – a far cry from today's coverage that splashed the image of a burning Grenfell Tower on every news stand with a promise of further coverage on a dozen more pages.

It was interesting to see how these tragic events were covered in the media as, despite the high death toll for a small area in many cases, coverage was still confined to just a few columns. The burning of the illegal clubs in London's Denmark Place was initially a well-covered horror story that soon fizzled out into barely any column inches at all. The pathetic coverage of a mass murder trial that should have been front-page news was nothing short of an outrage, and the lack of a memorial just as bad even today.

But what of the memorials? Of the twenty-three disasters here, only ten of them have some kind of memorial (some of them have more than one). This leaves so many with only the graves of the victims to be slowly covered over by greenery and eventually become unreadable with the weathering of the passing decades. How long before the last survivor or rescuer is alive to tell these stories? The Southampton fire in 1837 is too far past to know much about it. Nobody can recount the story or share the memories. We are left with a few pieces of paper and two stone slabs to prove this event ever took place.

Which begs the question – how many other disasters have shocked the country, or even the world, that we do not know about? While researching this book I was shocked to learn of the deaths of 183 children at the Victoria Hall in Sunderland in 1883, in a stampede that was not unlike the Barnsley disaster. For so many people, especially children, to be killed in such a short time, and with the death toll almost double that of the 1989 Hillsborough stadium disaster, and then essentially forgotten, means that we are in danger of forgetting so many more of these disasters as the years tick by.

But why are some tragedies remembered while others lay forgotten? We can safely say the modern-day media and sensational headlines have a role to play, but then, why did Denmark Place fade into history? And why do some tragedies – such as the deaths of the six Philpott children in Derby in 2011 – leave us all with the names of the killer more famous than any of the victims? The same goes for the New Cross fire – just months apart, two fires only a few miles away from one another, both devastating and wrapped in controversy, yet still a taboo subject in many ways.

The loss of a ship provides the reader with an image of a classic sailing vessel being dashed upon the rocks, or the countless retellings of the sinking of the *Titanic*, but for the crew of the *Gwendoline* and the *Flag Theofano*, their ships are no more heard of than many of the other 3 million lost ships around the world. Yet these two vessels today lie just a few miles off the British coast.

The thing about shipwrecks is that you can visualise a certain image when you hear a ship's name in your head – *Mary Rose, Titanic, Costa Concordia*. What if I said *Shadow V*? Would you recall the name of that vessel? What if I said five people died in an explosion on board her? Still nothing. But then if I said one of the five who died was Lord Mountbatten, suddenly everybody would remember the story of the uncle of Prince Philip and his family being blown up in a terrorist attack on the Irish coast. It is all about perspective and linking an incident with a memorable name; disasters that involve celebrities are more likely to stick in the mind.

Which leads me on to the subject of air disasters. Again, how many do you remember if you really think about it? There are dozens that have claimed the lives of celebrities but even their names fade with the birth of new generations. When film star Leslie Howard was killed during the Second World War he was mourned by the world who had loved his films, but how many know of him today? The start of the year 2020 saw the basketball star Kobe Bryant and eight others die in a helicopter crash, but how far down the line before he is just another Leslie Howard, great in his time, but not enough to be remembered fifty years later? It may be sad, but true.

What surprised me about the Dunkeswick air disaster was the fact that people who actually lived near the crash site in the field only fifteen years after the event had never heard of it. This did shock me, and I questioned what people talked about when something like that happened right on their doorstep. Does it then become a subject that is avoided? Do the next generation of residents fail to know the history of their village or town?

Although it was getting harder to conduct research due to the coronavirus pandemic, I paid a visit to the archives in Barnsley, where I was given access to the documents relating to the 1908 crush that led to sixteen children being killed. The building where this happened is right in the middle of the town centre, closed to visitors and looking unkempt. Sitting in a greasy spoon over the road, sipping on a cheap coffee from a chipped mug, I began to wonder how different it was 112 years ago. The people running out of the shop that I was now in, trying to help in any way they could, the parents and onlookers crowding the streets, looking to see what was going on. Although there are people who do genuinely care about this building and its history, there seems to be an ongoing battle to have others care in the same way; as I left, I spotted a blazing fire in the waste ground next to the building, started by a disreputable youth, and had to tell the theatre to call the fire brigade.

So where do I go from here? Well, this is not my first book on disasters: I have studied them for decades and as long as I can find enough information, I will carry on writing about them. An online blog has attracted numerous people who have come forward with information that would otherwise have been tucked away in a photo album, or stored in somebody's memory until the day when the incident is no longer relevant to anybody and simply becomes another statistic. This will not be my last book on such subjects; indeed, I have further projects planned, including ones on a lost landing craft from the 1982 Falklands conflict; a lost ship that has a popular namesake as a tourist boat; and a heroic resident of a seaside town who became the recipient of a rather prestigious award. But all this depends on whether enough information is out there, or indeed if there is enough interest in reading about it. Whatever happens, there is always a new subject to tackle.

There is so much more that I would have liked to include in this book but space just did not allow. The graves of the victims are something I always try to highlight, as well as how the scenes of the disasters look today and the people who risk their lives to help others facing certain death. The Hull rail crash is one of the subjects that I may tackle further. While writing this book, a host of never-before-seen photographs have come to my attention, as well as the location of many of the vicitims' last resting places – eleven out of twelve in Withernsea itself. An expedition to dive the wreck of the *Piłsudski* promises to show me the state it is in more than seventy years after its demise, and the modern street that is Hosier Lane today is another I plan to visit, but I see it in a different light now I know that it is the site of a mass murder that would be remembered for years to come.

Throughout the time spent studying these tragedies, I became aware of just how small some places are and how they have not changed in several generations. The small towns of Whitby and Sowerby Bridge and the village of Abbeystead have their own chequered pasts, the shocking events that took place there cementing their place in local history and in some cases providing a talking point that starts with 'do you remember?' or 'did you know?' depending on how much time has passed. In Whitby they are proud of the day their townsmen manned the lifeboat and saved several crews from wrecked ships, and their memory is now part of the town's celebration of the heroes of the storm, especially the lone survivor who went on to achieve so much more. The other side of Yorkshire sees the land-locked town of Sowerby Bridge being hit by two disasters, the tram crash in 1907 and the lorry accident in 1993. The fact that few residents of the town know about the tram crash proves that, without a memorial, history will not only be forgotten but it will inadvertently repeat itself.

The same goes for Dibbles Bridge. Who would have thought that a devastating bus crash would occur just two weeks before the fiftieth anniversary of the exact same thing happening? With a combined death toll of forty, this tiny stretch of road has killed more people than could be imagined, yet it seems there is little to stop it happening again. In my opinion, the site of Britain's worst road crash is just another accident waiting to happen, and it will only be a matter of time before there is another headline-hitting tragedy there.

I hope that I am wrong.

Acknowledgements

This book took many years to complete, as each disaster had to be meticulously researched and the story put together in order for it to read well and be truthful. This would not have been possible without a huge amount of help from the people who spent hours telling me their version of events, many of whom are still traumatised to this day.

Every effort has been made to trace all copyright holders to materials used. In the event of any omission, please contact me care of the publishers so that we may rectify for future editions

I would like to thank the following people:

1837: Southampton Fire

Southampton Reference Library
Steve Roberts

1861: Great Gale of Whitby

Neil Williamson, Curator at Whitby RNLI Lifeboat
  Museum Archive
Mike Major, Chairman of Whitby RNLI Lifeboat Management
  Group

1869: Hosier Lane Family Massacre

Stephanie Lyon

1893: Sinking of SS *Gwendoline*

Andrew Brighty
Ian Stubbs (Friends of Linthorpe Cemetery and Nature Reserve)

1907: Sowerby Bridge Tram

Lauren Brundell

1908: Barnsley Public Hall Crush

Kerena Mann
Barnsley Archives

1925: Dibbles Bridge Coach Crash (1)

Craven Herald (for the interview extracts and details)
Derek Smith
Basil Cardus
David Poole

1927: Hull Rail Disaster

Mike Covell
Mick Nicholson
Steve Bramley
Olwen Young

1939: Sinking of the *Piłsudski*

The National Archives, Kew

1952: Farnborough Air Show

Vic Prior
Ray Whincup

1957: Isle of Wight Air Crash

Marian Coghlan

1968: Ronan Point Collapse

Linda Pinder

1970: Explosion in the Hull Underpass

Nicola Carter
Tony Wilkinson
Becka Rose Ward
Dorothy Ward
Rosemary Campey

1971: Clarkston Gas Explosion

Chris MacInnes
Robert Allan
Elaine Graham
Karen Lund

1975: Dibbles Bridge Coach Crash (2)

Derek Smith
Stephen Dobson
Eileen Dobson
Kevin Hullah
Basil Cardus

1976: Fire on HMS *Glasgow*

Leonard Henry
Denis Pratt
John Harris
Alexander Crawford
Tom Lyall
Kenneth Hyland

1980: Denmark Place Arson Attack

Dave Pare

1981: New Cross Fire

John Taylor
George Thompson
Arthur Wilson

1984: Abbeystead Explosion

Jean Grubb
Gill Ellison
Matthew Scott
Francis O'Neill
Angela Rothwell

1985: Dover Hovercraft Crash

John Kobam
Geoff Delivett

1990: Sinking of the *Flag Theofano*

Roger Thornton
Martin Woodward
Ian Grove

1993: Southampton Airport Crash

Adrian Walder
Martin Cole

1995: Knight Air Flight 816 Crash

Sue Scott, for giving me
a tape of *Close Up North*
Cllr Richard Thomas
Anthony Hunt
David Griffiths
David Rayner
Elizabeth Snowden
Florence Walker
John Waller

Keith Elliott
Michael Webster
Neil Duffy
Paul Kernaghan
North Yorkshire Police
Jon Wornham (for his
photograph of G-OEAA)
Andrew Budimir

There are so many more people who could be named here who assist my research in the smallest of ways but they have such a big impact. For that I thank you also.

Finally, I would like to say a big thanks to my wife, Juliette. Without her love and support during my writing and research phase I would not get half of the things done that I want in the time that I do them. Here's to another successful project.

The destination for history
www.thehistorypress.co.uk